6/01

WOMEN

| BY |

WOMEN

Also edited by Tori Haring-Smith

Monologues for Women by Women
More Monologues for Women by Women
Scenes for Women by Women

EVEN MORE

MONOLOGUES

FOR

WOMEN

BY

WOMEN

EDITED BY TORI HARING-SMITH

HEINEMANN
Portsmouth, NH

Heinemann
A division of Reed Elsevier Inc.
361 Hanover Street
Portsmouth, NH 03801–3912
www.heinemanndrama.com

Offices and agents throughout the world

Performance rights information can be found on page 160.

Library of Congress Cataloging-in-Publication Data
Even more monologues for women by women / edited by Tori Haring-Smith.

    p. cm.
    Includes index.
    ISBN 0-325-00247-9
    1. Monologues. 2. Acting. 3. American drama—20th century.
4. American drama—Women authors. 5. Women—Drama.
I. Haring-Smith, Tori.

PN2080 .M5475 2001
812'.04508952042—dc21

                                 00-040875

Editor: Lisa A. Barnett
Production: Elizabeth Valway
Cover design: Tom Allen, Pear Graphic Design
Manufacturing: Louise Richardson

Printed in the United States of America on acid-free paper
04 03 02 01 00 DA 1 2 3 4 5

Contents

Subject Index

Sibling and Family Relationships

O'Connor, Sleepwalkers
Ryan, Cigarette
Slugocki, Wild Fire

Social Expectations

Adamson, Doppelganger
Appel, Sorry
Kahn, Summer in the City
Kramer, The Law Makes Evening Fall
Kuper, Indecent Exposure
Maslowski, I Know Me

Technology

Korotkin, That's Another Story, Dot Com
Leavitt, Good Vibrations
Plumb, Fruct

Urban Life and Materialism

Cizmar, Street Stories
Kahn, Summer in the City
Neipris, Southernmost Tip
Ryan, Cigarette

Introduction

Thoughts on Women, Theatre, and a New Millennium

In 1998 Paula Vogel won the Pulitzer Prize for Drama. In 1999 it was Margaret Edson. Two women in a row. Women account for 40 percent of students in M.F.A. playwriting programs, more than 50 percent of M.F.A. acting students, and more than 60 percent of theatre ticket buyers. In September 1998, *American Theatre* magazine ran a special issue on "Women in Theatre" highlighting the work of writers, designers, managers, and actresses. Julie Taymor's adaptation of *The Lion King* has brought a new and more sophisticated sensibility to Broadway. Things should be looking up for women in theatre.

Yet, despite all this good press, it is still true that less than 20 percent of the plays produced in America are written by women, and many of those works are designated as "theatre for young people." In fact, only in the area of children's entertainment are women's plays produced as often as men's. It seems clear that a play written by a woman is still considered "just a woman's play" with a limited audience, while a play written by a man is, well, a play. And in this time of reduced funding for the arts, theatres remain conservative in their season selections. More classics. More "sure bets." More of those plays by men that are assumed to have universal appeal. Is it any wonder that The Guerrilla Girls have been putting up signs in theatre restrooms reading: "In this theatre the taking of photographs, the use of recording devices, and the production of plays by women are strictly prohibited." (Quoted in Alisa Solomon's "Steal This Stage: The State of Women in Theatre 1999," *Village Voice*, May 19–25, 1999.)

This collection of work is designed for actresses who want to inhabit women characters created by women. These characters are not easy to find. Because women's plays are not widely produced, they are not widely published either. Even when editors collect monologues for women, usually 60–80 percent of the selections are written by men. How does this reluctance to publish and produce women's plays affect actresses? Surely male playwrights have created some wonderful roles for women: Shakespeare's Portia, Tennessee Williams' Blanche DuBois, Eugene O'Neill's Mary Tyrone, Oscar Wilde's Lady Bracknell. But these women are inevitably created from an outsider's perspective. The creators are great playwrights in large part because they are such acute observers of human behavior. But they are still outsiders. They see mothers through the eyes of a son. They see women's sexuality in relationship to their own. They have not lived inside a woman's skin. This situation is exacerbated by the fact that so many theatre directors are men. Far too many actresses find themselves in rehearsal trying to embody a female character who was created by a male playwright and is being interpreted by a male director. For many actresses it can be refreshing to speak words written by someone who shares their gender with them—who writes female characters from an insider's perspective. It is important for them to be able to take on the roles of women who were created by other women, who can become, quite literally, "role models." To address this concern, we have added a third volume to our series of *Monologues for Women by Women*.

Of course not all women are alike. We grow and change from age twenty to forty to sixty. Race and class can shape our lives and our experiences as much as gender can. A homeless white woman sees life very differently than an Asian-American corporate lawyer. A straight Roman Catholic mother of five experiences life differently than her lesbian Quaker neighbor. We are all individuals. But gender does shape our lives in profound ways from the moment we are born ("Did she have a boy or a girl?"). And since we learn how to interpret our lives and how to shape our futures from the stories we hear, it is important that we hear stories told from the inside.

Like the first two volumes in this series, this collection of monologues features a wide range of voices and characters. There are young women dealing with breast cancer, older women reflecting on lifelong marriages, lesbians, single mothers, students, a fishing guide, a commercial model, a political revolutionary, a mathematician, and a woman who has a penis. The women who speak from these pages are concerned about violence, religion, disintegrating families, the feminist movement, the pain of underwire bras, the emotional life of crabs, and their own inability to feel emotion.

Similarly, the writers represented here have varied backgrounds. Some have spent most of their lives raising a family, others devote their time to their careers outside of the home. Some are primarily novelists, others screenwriters, and still others do most of their work for the stage. Some of the writers represented here are students, others are retired. Some are widely produced, others are new voices. Some are adamantly political, others eschew politics as much as possible. Some live in New York and others in small communities in the South. And that is what makes the collection so exciting—its characters grow out of the rich panoply of women's experiences.

This third volume in the *Monologues for Women by Women* series is a little different than its two predecessors, however, in that it has works by women from the United Kingdom, Australia, New Zealand, and Germany, as well as from the United States. As the Internet weaves our world closer together and makes English a global lingua franca, it provides ways for women around the world to share their concerns. Our dialects differ a bit, but we address the same concerns that have been women's issues for centuries: motherhood, relationships, aging, spirituality, health, and sexuality. And for all of us, theatre provides a way to speak our minds, to raise these concerns for public discussion. In short, there is a whole world of women in these pages. I hope you will help us move it from the page to the stage. Enjoy!

Tips on Auditioning with a Monologue

Choosing a Monologue

In order to perform a monologue well, you should have some personal connection to it. You need to understand the character's emotion, and be passionate about her concerns. After all, you are going to have to explore this character in depth and then generate enough energy to make her live for your audience. In some cases, actors are drawn to monologue characters because they have undergone similar experiences. If the character is talking about death, and you have recently lost a loved one, you may be able to share something of yourself—your grief—through bringing the character to life. Remember, acting is about sharing yourself. That's one reason why actors must learn to be vulnerable and to relax. When you audition, your audience wants to know who you are, as well as who you can be. Your choice of a monologue often reveals you, so choose carefully.

It is common advice that monologues should talk about the present, not just recount memories from the past. I think this advice, while well-intentioned, is artificially limiting. There is nothing wrong with a monologue that tells a story from the past as long as you, the actor, make it present and active. As long as the story is a vital part of the character you develop, it will stir emotions, shape interactions, and reveal layers within the character. Remember that all monologues have at least one silent stage partner, someone who is listening and responding to the character, perhaps driving the character to keep speaking. Sometimes the silent partner is another character, sometimes another facet of the speaker, and sometimes the theatre audience. As long as a monologue connects with your passions, you will be able to make it live for your silent stage partner and for your audience.

Even though a monologue springs from the interaction of two characters, it must not be too dependent on the context of the play if it is going stand on its own in an audition. That is, the monologue needs to make sense and be important in its own right—not because of its function within the play as a whole. Many of the most exciting monologues in full-length plays simply cannot stand on their own, because in isolation they do not reveal the character fully enough. Most successful audition monologues do not refer to too many people other than the speaker. It's difficult to keep track of a woman's lover, husband, daughter, and business associate all in a single two-minute monologue! The primary purpose of a monologue is to showcase you, not the play or the playwright. If a monologue is well chosen, it should not require any introduction beyond the title of the play.

It is important that a monologue (or a pair of monologues, if you are performing two together) allow you to show a range of emotional, physical, and vocal qualities. While you can get some range by choosing a pair of contrasting monologues, each piece you do should have variety within it. The emotional state of the character needs to be dynamic, so that you can show how the character develops through shifts in your voice, posture, gestures, and movement. If you are choosing a pair of monologues, you will probably want to find speeches with different subjects as well as differing tones.

When choosing a monologue, you should try to find material that will be new to your audience. When I audition large numbers of people, I hear the same monologues over and over again. Sometimes I can hardly force myself to listen to painfully familiar pieces like the twirler from *In the Boom-Boom Room*. When you choose a classical monologue, think about how many Juliets or Kates your auditioners will have heard on the professional stage and in auditions. Try to find some new material. Women playwrights from the Middle

Ages, the Renaissance, the Restoration, and the eighteenth century are just now being rediscovered and published. Look for anthologies of their works, and you may find wonderful new monologues. Although this collection will not help you find a classical monologue, it will provide you with more than fifty previously unpublished or very hard-to-find contemporary pieces.

Finally, be sure that the monologue is suitable for you as well as for the theatre or film for which you are auditioning. This does not mean that the character needs to match you identically in race, gender, age, or geographical location. Just be sure that you understand the character and how she responds to life. If you feel that you would respond as she does, you probably have a sympathetic relationship to the character. If you are playing someone much older or younger than yourself, do not "play age"—play yourself. Also avoid pieces that require a strong accent, unless you are told that you need to demonstrate particular dialect abilities. Some people have an accented piece in their storehouse of "extra" monologues—those that are not their primary audition pieces but are available if the auditioners want to see more.

Think about the suitability of your monologue for the medium in which you are auditioning. If you are being seen for television work, the monologue should be rated "PG." If you have been called for a particular role, try to find a monologue that is generally linked to that script or role (i.e., use a comic piece if you're auditioning for a comedy), but is not from the script itself. The auditioners will have all kinds of preconceived notions about the roles they are casting. If you pull a monologue from the play they have been dreaming about for several months, you may not seem right to them if your interpretation of the character does not match their ideal for it. If the auditioners want to see you in the part, they will ask for a cold reading.

Finally, think about the length of your monologues. Do not cram so much into your two or three minutes that you feel rushed while you are performing. Respect the time limits set by the auditioners. Some of the monologues in this book are obviously too long to be done in an audition, and you will have to cut them. But having access to the entire monologue gives you a fuller sense of context as well as offering you material for longer performances in showcases and workshops.

Preparing and Rehearsing

As you rehearse your monologue, either alone or with a coach, use the techniques that have been most successful for you in preparing full-length roles. If the piece is from a longer work, read that play. But do not rely on the longer work to "explain" the character—after all, your auditioners may not know the piece. The monologue must stand on its own as a comprehensible piece, telling the auditioners all they need to know about your character. Also, don't let the full play's context limit you. Don't assume that because the character in the play is insane, your interpretation must also reveal insanity.

More important than any research in the library, more important even than reading the full script, is careful examination of the specific text that you are going to present. Think about the character drawn there and ask yourself the usual character-development questions, including:

- Who is this person talking to? Does that shift at any point during the piece? What does the listener want from the speaker?
- What question or event is the speaker responding to? What happened just before she began to speak?
- What does the speaker need? Why does she keep on speaking? (Make this need as important as possible.)
- What are the conflicts within the speaker and between the speaker and her listener(s)?
- What does the speaker's language reveal about her? What is the speaker's favorite word in this monologue?

- How is the speaker different after she has said her piece than before? What has she gained, lost, discovered?
- What line in the monologue is the most important? Where does the speech make emotional turns? Where does it reach a climax?

As you explore the character, keep reassuring yourself, that you are not necessarily looking for the "right" answers to your character questions. You are looking for emotionally truthful answers that you can play. Be faithful to your own experience and your own sense of truth—not to what someone else thinks that the character "should" be like. Do not be satisfied with quick, easy answers. Keep probing.

As you work on the character, consider her vocal and physical life. Would she sit down, or is she too overwrought? Does she try to hide her strong emotions behind civilized, controlled speech, or does she speak out? Experiment with different business you might give the character as well. Is she knitting while she talks? Is she fidgeting with a button? Putting on makeup? Consider her body stance. Does she stand tall? Hunch forward? Sit primly? Be sure to make choices that allow you to keep your head up and that do not force you to move so frenetically that the auditioners cannot "see" you for the movement. Know where your silent partner is. Do not make the auditioner a silent partner—no one wants to be forced to participate in an actor's piece. Does the silent partner move at any point? Where, when, and how?

As you rehearse, concentrate on your primary goal of making the character present and active. Command attention—think of what Linda Loman says about Willy— "Attention must be paid." If you know what the character wants, then you will have no trouble bringing out that need for the audience.

Once you begin to put your actual performance together, consider how you will start. Your introduction of yourself and your piece are part of the performance, because you are, in fact, "on" from the moment that you walk through the doors of the audition room or onto the stage. Practice introducing yourself pleasantly and efficiently:

> Hello. My name is _____, and today I'll be doing monologues from Caridad Svich's *Prodigal Kiss* and Mary Pix's *The Innocent Mistress*.

Then work on the transition into your first monologue. Take a moment to visualize your character's situation, to ground yourself in her needs, to place your silent partner, and to think about the question or event that you are responding to. Practice this kind of preparation, and you will not need more than five to ten seconds to accomplish it.

Work through the transitions between monologues in the same way. After you have chosen an order for your pieces, consider how you will move smoothly from one to the other. Be sure that you complete the first monologue, give it a beat to sink in, then alter your physicality in some way, and quickly launch into the second piece. As you rehearse, have someone time your work. Be sure that you are well within the time limits set by the audition. When you are performing, you want to be able to think about the character, not the clock. Take your time to live the character fully but not self-indulgently. And, above all, don't be afraid of being boring. If you think you're boring, you're going to telegraph that to your auditioners, and your worst nightmare will come true.

Plan what you are going to wear to the audition. Think of something that complements your body type and doesn't distort your presentation of either of your characters. You do not want to look costumed during your audition; you want to look as much like yourself as you can. The goal of the audition is to reveal yourself and the range of your abilities. You may want to costume a character by adding or taking off a jacket or scarf, but do not plan elaborate costume changes. Most people do not change costume at all during their auditions. After all, you should be able to present the character without relying on a costume to support you. Similarly, you may need one small prop in one of your monologues—a pencil, a book. If you need more props than that, you have not chosen an appropriate audition piece. Remember that the only furniture you will probably have available is a chair. Try to be as self-sufficient as possible, and not to rely on costumes, props, or furniture. Your acting—not the technical aspects of your performance—must be the focus. Your auditioners should remember you, not your costume.

As you rehearse, keep exploring. Take risks—that's what rehearsals are for. If you find that you are afraid of looking foolish—playing either too big or too small—face your fears. Do the monologue as you fear it might be seen at its very worst. Facing your fears helps dissolve them away. But if you don't face them, enact them, and experience your worst nightmare in the safety of a rehearsal, your fears will limit your spontaneity and make you censor yourself. Sometimes, you will discover that your worst nightmare may have been an excellent choice for the piece—you were just afraid of taking the chance. Don't be afraid to be quirky or bold.

Some people hire coaches to help them prepare monologue work. Whether you rehearse alone or with a coach, at some point you need to practice performing your work in front of different audiences. Don't always practice or perform in the same studio. Move around. Get used to performing anywhere, so that the strangeness of the audition situation will not throw you. If you can perform with equal concentration and comfort in a living room, on a stage, in a classroom, and out of doors, you're probably well prepared for your audition.

Presenting Yourself and Your Work

Before your audition, try not to establish expectations. Of course, you should be aware of any rules that have been set for the audition—the number of pieces you should present, time limits, requirements for the types of monologues—but don't establish expectations for the audition process itself. Don't "picture" the room, because you may be surprised, and then you'll have to deal with that surprise when you should be acting. If you think, "Oh, I'll be up on a big stage in a two-thousand-seat auditorium," and you end up auditioning in a hotel conference room, you'll have trouble making immediate adjustments, and doing so will distract you from concentrating on the monologue.

Don't even make assumptions about the behavior or the number of the people who will be watching you. Sometimes you will be performing for one person, sometimes for fifty or sixty in combined auditions such as Strawhat or Midwest Theatre Auditions. Don't anticipate rapt attention from your auditors. They may look at you intently, they may eat while you perform (they often don't get lunch breaks), or they may pass papers around or talk about you. Don't be surprised, don't be thrown. Just do your work and let them do theirs. It is hard not to be offended if someone is talking while you perform, but keep your concentration on your own work. Remember, they may be saying, "She's perfect for the part, isn't she?"

Get a good night's sleep before your audition and wear comfortable clothes. If you're going on a callback, wear the same or similar clothes that you wore to the first audition. If the auditioners liked that person, they will both remember and like a similar looking one during callbacks. Wearing a T-shirt and jeans to an initial audition and then a suit to the callbacks only confuses the people who are trying to find the real you. Bring extra copies of your picture and resume in case you need them.

Know where you are going and give yourself plenty of time to get there. You don't want to be nervous about your punctuality. You may have forms to fill out, and you will want to warm up before you audition. Find a quiet space to center yourself, warm up vocally and physically, and run over your piece to be sure that you are comfortable with it. If you can't find a private space, just close your eyes, focus, and take yourself through the piece in your head. Follow the emotional track of the character and visualize your silent partner. In other words, perform in your head. This is the same practice that professional athletes engage in when they visualize themselves making a free throw or kicking a goal before they act.

When it is time for you to audition, you will be admitted into the audition room by a monitor or the casting director. In most cases, you or the casting director will have sent your picture and resume to the director. If not, then hand the picture and resume to the director as you enter the room and cross to the audition area. If the director initiates a conversation, respond politely and efficiently. Think of this as a cocktail conversation. Most directors, though, will not initiate conversation. They're rushed, and they just want to see who you are.

As soon as you enter the room, seize the space. Walk confidently and know that for the next three minutes, you are in charge of what happens in that space. It is all too easy to experience auditions as a kind of meat market in which you are just a number. In fact, auditions are often like this, but you must never present yourself as "just one more actor." Take the stage. Know you're important.

If you need to move a chair or set up the space, do so quickly. Then pause to be sure that the director is ready for you to proceed. In some cases, a monitor will indicate when you should begin. Introduce yourself and your piece, making eye contact with the director or with as many of a large group of directors as possible. This is the only time during the formal part of the audition that you should make direct eye contact with the auditioners. Set up your space so that you are facing the auditioners, but put your silent partner to one side of them or just behind them. Once your introduction is over, take a few seconds (no more) to focus completely on your work and then go.

At the end of the performance, wait a beat, break character, and then say, "Thank you." If, for some reason, the director wants to see more of you, you may be asked to do a cold reading or additional monologues. Always have some additional work in reserve. It is not uncommon, especially in graduate school auditions, for directors to request specific types of monologues. "Do you have something more upbeat?" "Can you show us a more vulnerable character?" "Do you have something in verse?" You can never be prepared for all requests, but have a supply of work at your beck and call. If you are not asked to do additional work, however, don't be depressed. You may not suit the role, or you may be so perfect that the auditioners know immediately they want to see you at callbacks.

When you've finished, never comment on your own work—especially to apologize. The most important thing is to be confident and to look like you're having a good time throughout the ordeal. Don't even comment on your own work by scowling, frowning, or shrugging as you walk away.

Once you have left the audition, try not to second-guess the director. Even if the director seemed to respond well to your work, don't begin to fantasize about what it will be like to work with that director or on that project. If you don't get the part, you'll just be doubly disappointed. Every actor needs a strong support system. You put yourself on the line daily—you are the product that you are selling—and although you may know that not everyone wants or needs your product, it is never easy to take rejection. Remember that even famous actors face rejection every day. Keeping faith in yourself and in those around you who stay by you in your times of need will sustain you and keep you sane.

Auditioning can be a nightmare, but it can also be fun. You meet lots of different people, get tips on upcoming projects, and have a chance, however brief, to perform. Just keep reminding yourself that you are in control of your performance. No matter how good you are, you will only be right for some roles. Can you imagine Roseanne Barr as a sensitive figure skater? Keep true to your own sense of self, keep polishing your acting skills, and be sure that you have other ways of measuring your self-worth aside from getting cast in any one given role.

Doppelganger

JO J. ADAMSON

(The model is standing on the deck of a cruise ship as the photographer approaches her.)

MODEL: A thousand things go through my head as the photographer checks the light. Is my lipstick glossy? Cheeks luminous? Figure voluptuous? Eyes bright, teeth pearly? Hair curly? Will I project the correct image? *(Trying different poses)* Vacationing? Young Miss Contemplating? Ingenue Visits Atlanta. Society Deb. On Verandah. Young Beauty Soaks up Sun. American Miss Visits Venice. Austrian Lass Studies Sunset. Fraulein Heinler Smiles at Photographer. Mademoiselle Cline Boards Luxury Liner. *(Photographer adjusts his equipment while she powders her nose.)* Focus your lens on my tight skin. I was born for the close-up. The sun is my friend: I open like a flower. Come to me. Come *on*. Photograph the light around my cells. The shadow of my smile. Soft focus me to the edge of eternity. I'm the infinite closing of your iris shot. The particle in your eye that won't wash out. Feel me to the whorls of your fingers. Preserve the dream emulsion in your soul. Embalm the celluloid daylights out of me and I'll look good in tomorrow's photogravure. *(Trying different poses again)* How do you want me? It's a rhetorical question. Fetching? Perhaps. Whimsical, capricious, coquettish, to be sure. Here's Pert, Saucy, Bewitching . . . Alluring. I give you Tantalizing, Teasing, Tempting, always. Toss of head, angle of chin, curve of neck always right up to the orgasmic dissolve. *(Addressing the photographer)* We work well together. Where do you stop and I begin? I await your separation in safe-light suspension. OK, I'm ready. Click the shutter. *(She becomes flustered, unsure.)* I'm all aflutter. You'd think I'd be used to this. Each time is like the first virgin thrust. One more minute, my makeup's running, nose shiny . . . No! I'm beauty's perfection, the stuff dreams are made of. "No sweat" as they say. Click the shutter while the feeling rises. Take the wave at its crest. Now! Fire when ready, sir. I'm at my best.

Sorry

DORI APPEL

(Theresa Barnes, a woman in her late thirties, speaks from a ward in a mental hospital, addressing the audience as though speaking to fellow patients. Throughout the monologue, moments of forthrightness and humor vie with those of confusion, despair, and rage.)

THERESA: Two o'clock. Free time on the funny farm, everybody, and I suggest you spend it with me. It will do you more good than watching the soaps, more good than the Tuesday afternoon sing-a-long, more good than chair caning class. Chair caning! Where did they think up that one? We're mentally ill, not blind!

Hey, you ever think about how you got crazy? Or do you just imagine that the little gears inside your brain just somehow jumped the track? I think about it a lot. That's one thing about being in this place, you get some time to think. And I'll tell you something—I believe being crazy may be the final and perfect expression of what we've been trained for all our lives.

Think of it this way—what's the thing we say the most? Come on, girlfriends, help me out. *(She points.)* Right! "I'm sorry." Whatever it is, whoever's upset, it's something for you to apologize for. You drank the last Pepsi, or the dog peed on the rug, or your husband lost his keys, or your kid didn't get invited to somebody's party, or it rained or it didn't, and it seems like you ought to say, "I'm sorry."

And what's everybody say to us when *we're* upset? *(She points.)* You got it—"It's all in your head." If they hurt your feelings, you're too sensitive—it's all in your head. If they make you mad, they didn't mean anything—it's all in your head. If you get scared, there's nothing to be afraid of—it's all in your head. And the backaches and night sweats and stomach and skin problems that don't ring the right bells on the medical testing machines, they're in your head, too. *(Beat)* And so now we're crazy, and *everything* bothers us, and it's *all* in our heads, and we're really sorry to boot!

(In a reproving and slightly condescending voice) "It's a sickness like any other sickness, Mrs. Barnes. There's nothing to be ashamed of." *(In her own voice)* That's the social worker, who has, of course, already read every humiliating detail of why you need to be here. No shame, no blame, and no reason to think that anyone stuck you in this place just to shut you up. *(In the reproving and reasoning voice)* "The hospital is just a little time-out."

(In her own voice) Sure, why not? I put my kids in time-out sometimes. When they're *bad*. And I tell them it's for their own good. You put the bad kid in the room and you say, "You have to stay there until you can behave yourself." And then you shut the door. *(Beat)* Stay right there, crazy lady, until you can remember how to be . . . a lady. The job description's pinned to the back of the closed door.

But somewhere there's a bad little girl who isn't afraid of being left alone in that dark room. She'd just sit there, and when her husband came—oh no, that's no good. *(She laughs.)* Little girls don't have husbands, do they? *(Beat)* Woe be to the one who does not emerge from the closed room remorseful, who will not say "Sorry" when they finally let her out. They've got the evidence: the buckets of tears, the meals not cooked, kids not cared for, husbands suffering from insufficient screwing. *(Beat)* Evidence. Evidence. The groove worn in the mattress during the sleeping days, the varnish worn off the floor during the nonsleeping, pacing nights. The razor blades, the empty bottles of pills. *(Beat)* Sorry. I'm sorry. Love, honor, obey, and be sorry.

You want to know why they sent me here? Just because I stopped being sorry and started getting— Well, it was clear

4

that I wasn't myself. A woman in her right mind doesn't scream like a banshee at the drop of a hat, and break every dish in the kitchen cabinets, and cut all the cords off the household appliances. My husband was annoyed, of course. But he worries about me, he wants me to get well—and the staff is very encouraging. The very first day I was here, I was sitting on the bed and watching my sad-looking feet hanging down, and that nurse with the big, round, smiley face came in with a lunch tray. She gave me an extra big smile as she set it down, and told me how I was going to be back on my feet real soon. I knew what she meant. *(As the nurse, with the voice of an evil witch)* "You're going to be cooking and cleaning and jumping to meet everybody's whim and demand before you've even caught your breath! The moment your insurance runs out, you're gone!" *(As herself, rather matter-of-fact)* After I threw the custard from the lunch tray in her face, I learned about a new version of time-out: The Quiet Room. Nothing in it but a mattress on the floor. While I was locked up in there, I thought about what I'd done. It wasn't nice. So I wrote "Sorry" on the wall with my own shit.

Then on the weekend my husband Sandy came, looking some combination of miserable and guilty, and he told me how he and the kids missed me and wanted me home. And I really was sorry. I wasn't angry anymore, and I cried all the rest of the day, and everybody here started being much nicer to me. When the doctor came to see me, he told me that a lot of women these days are angry about their roles. "Well," I said, "Maybe they've been given a stale one."

He kept on talking, of course, but I didn't listen. I was thinking about the Quiet Room when they locked me in there. Only it was different. It wasn't that bare room with the mattress that I was thinking about. It was a little girl's bedroom, all frilly blue and white. *(She drifts into her fantasy.)* A little girl is being sent to her room for being bad. She can't come out until she's sorry. They close the door, and as soon as they're gone, she hops off the bed and crouches down so she can see under it. She picks up the blue organdy ruffle that matches the curtains and pillow shams that her Mommy and Daddy got her because she's their special little girl, and she reaches under there and hauls out a big old ax! She runs her finger over the blade carefully, just to make sure it's sharp. And then, SMASH! There go all the nice storybooks, and the dollhouse with its tiny furniture, and SMASH! There goes the white painted dresser holding her neatly folded clothes, and the bed posts off the bed. And SMASH! She chops down that closed door and she bursts out free! And she tells everyone, "I'm not sorry! Not one bit!" *(Shaken, she returns to the present and regains control, though she is still in the grip of strong emotion. She glances at her watch.)* Free hour's just about up, isn't it? That person from the community college is supposed to come and tell us about all their adult noncredit courses. I doubt that they've got the one I want. What I want is a course on the social history of apology. I want know the origins of the word "Sorry." That's what I want to study, and I want it for credit. Full credit.

Street Stories

PAULA CIZMAR

(Elise, a woman in her late twenties or early thirties, runs on a street in mid-city Los Angeles.)

ELISE: So I'm running.
Plap, plap, plap, plap.
Shit. Plap, plap, plap.
Sucks sucks sucks.
Fuck this, man.
Plap, plap.
And let me tell you, ain't nothing good about it.

I'm running, what? Two years? Three? Let me tell you: it never gets any easier. I'm doing it and the whole time I'm beating a drum inside. I hate this, just don't stop, I hate this, just don't stop, I hate this. I never look forward to it, I never like it, I never get second wind, I never get to that so-called place, that laughable place, that runner's high when you lose yourself or your sense of what you're doing and oh, sure, truly merge with the movement. Yeah right. Time never passes automatically. Unconsciously. I never find myself miraculously somewhere else, a mile down the road, having passed through here already, having passed through invisible timeless space, having gotten lost in the moment, ending up elsewhere. A long ways away. No. That does not happen. And I honestly don't think it ever will.

Yeah. And I don't need to do this for my health. And I don't need to do this for my weight. And I don't need to do this, period. You want me to make you sick? I'll confess: I'm one of these people who can eat any damned thing—any-thing—as much as I want any time of the day or night. You

7

want a bacon cheddar cheeseburger at midnight? Give it to me to eat it for you. And your fries, too. Won't matter a damn. Always been that way.

But I'm running. And I pass every broken down lot, every wasted car plastered together with duct tape, bobby pins, "I love Tepatitlan" stickers, every cracked retaining wall sprouting rat-choke ivy, every hole, every scratch, every last one.

I pass the house with the three rotten-breath terriers bouncing off the screen, and the hopeful house where some optimist is trying to grow grass in the soot layer she calls a backyard, and a volunteer tomato near a mildewed brown couch someone threw out six months ago. I pass one, no two, finally three Von's shopping carts rolled on their side, and a mylar windmill stuck in a dead rock garden, and three plastic ducks, and a red, a pink, a yellow plastic kiddie chair, and a chrome globe on a pyramid, and door . . . door . . . door . . . each door hiding a bigger loss than the next.

I pass the ageless boy who sits alone in his wheelchair all day, under an overgrown ficus, unable to call anybody 'cause he can only talk with a pointer held in his mouth aimed at a letter, his magic voice, a Ouija board, and I pass the convalescent home and shut my ears and try not to picture powder blue or plastic basins, and run past the ambulance, no lights flashing, no big rush, pulling into the lot.

I pass the land of flowers where an old Norwegian planted anything he could get his hands on in obsessive little rows and across the street a black schoolteacher re-created his auntie's yard in Mississippi. I know this 'cause he told me. And I pass the place where the crack dealers moved to, as if the cops don't know. There's a pay phone out front.

And I run past all of it 'cause I don't have to know any of this.
I run past it 'cause I can.
So I'm running.
And running isn't anywhere.

Epiphany

HEIDI DECKER

(Woman, 20–30. Articulates well, but speaks as if everything is one continuous thought and sentence. Not ditzy by any means, only genuinely perplexed. She has been up for hours, mulling something over. She speaks aloud to try to make some sense of it all.)

All right, maybe I'm just losin' it. It's not unheard of, these days, for someone to just lose it for no apparent reason. Maybe that's it. Either that or I've had some deeply symbolic, spiritual experience and I just didn't get it. I don't know.

All I know is that now, I can't get it out of my head. It's just there, right behind my eyes, and it won't leave me alone.

Don't get me wrong, I'm not obsessed or anything. It's just that I feel like the whole thing is supposed to . . . I don't know . . . *tell* me something.

I know how really dumb that sounds. I just wonder if this is one of those experiences that you read about . . . things that don't hardly ever happen, and when you try to explain it, out loud, it sounds really dumb, but in some weird way it can change your life . . . sorta.

See, last night I was leaving work, it was about ten o'clock at night, and I was hungry but I didn't have very much money. I decided to go to the grocery store because it's open 'til midnight and they have a deli section where they have fresh sandwiches made every day and after nine o'clock at night they mark them half price 'cause they have to get rid of them 'cause they can't sell them the next day . . . because they're advertised to be made fresh every day. So, you can get a really big sandwich for a dollar.

Then I began walking across the back part of the store to the dairy section to get some milk. I was walking along, trying to decide whether I wanted skim or two percent, when something in the seafood section caught my eye.

You know how a lot of grocery stores have a big tank with lobsters in it? And there's usually about a dozen all piled in there, with rubber bands wrapped around their claws so they can't snap at anyone, or defend themselves or anything . . .

Well, last night there weren't any lobsters. One tank was empty, and the other had seven or eight crabs in it. Big ones. Kind of like soft-shell but not exactly . . . maybe they were snow crabs . . . you know, with those *huge* front claws that you see people in restaurants pounding on with a hammer.

Apparently these guys were a specialty item running for a few days.

What caught my eye was this: all those crabs were huddled over in one corner, looking like they were trying to keep warm or play king of the mountain or something . . . all but one. One of them was way far away from the others. He was sitting right at the edge of the tank, pressed up against the glass, and, I swear to God, *watching what was going on in the store.* Like a little kid with his hands pressed against the glass watching some guy toss pizza crust.

Well, there's no one around but me, so I was the only thing moving . . . and . . . you know how they have those little eyes on top of their heads?

Every time I moved, they would *follow* me. Back and forth, up and down. Now that's not so strange. I'm sure had he been in the ocean he would have been watching whatever happened to be moving.

I stepped up close to the glass and I guess it kind of startled him because his eyes disappeared into his head for a few seconds, but I stood there and slowly his eyes came back out. I bent down a little bit and put my hand up to the glass.

It was really cold outside and I still had my gloves on. I'm crouched down next to a lobster tank with my hand up against the glass watching this crab watch me, when I heard someone pushing a shopping cart pass by me.

The noise made me remember where I was and I stood up quickly, and as I did, the crab's eyes ducked back down into his head. I stood there for a few seconds, waiting, but they didn't come back out again.

I noticed that my hands were getting sweaty so I took off my gloves and as I did, I happened to look at my watch and saw that it was getting late. I started to walk away when . . . I *swear* . . . I heard a little . . . tapping . . . noise.

I looked back, and that crab was tapping the glass with one of his claws. He was lifting one of his front claws a little and tapping steadily on the glass. I'd never seen anything like it. Well, who has? So I crouched down again to get a closer look.

He just kept . . . tapping . . . until finally I put my fingers against the glass, right in the spot where he was tapping. He stopped. He just left his claw there on the glass.

I tapped my fingers, twice, against the glass. *He tapped back. Twice!* I *swear*. I tapped once. He tapped once. I don't even know why I think it was a he, I just do.

And then . . . and *then*, I put my other hand against the glass. And waited. And slowly, he lifted his other claw, and put it against the glass, opposite of where my hand was.

So I'm in the middle of this grocery store, crouched down nose to nose with the daily under-the-sea special and . . .

. . . and for a second . . . I swear to you, for a second . . . I . . . felt . . . something.

I don't know what. I know it sounds ridiculous but he had his claws against my hands and my eyes were level with his, with just half an inch of glass between us and for a second I felt . . . *something* . . . right in the middle of my chest. Not like heartburn or anything, just, sort of, I don't know . . . warm. I guess. I could feel it on my skin, but inside too . . . kind of like a . . . glow. Just for a second.

Then he brought his claws back down. He backed away

and turned away a little, then stopped, and kind of looked at me . . . then turned himself around and crawled to the back of the tank. I just crouched there and watched him, half expecting him to turn and wave, with a sunset shimmering behind him.

By now my knees were killing me so I stood up, kinda shaky. I left the sandwich I was going to buy there, on the floor, and walked out of the store. Out in the parking lot it was freezing cold, but I could still feel that . . . whatever it was . . . it was the strangest feeling. I got in my car and went home. I was in kind of a daze, I guess.

And so now, I can't get it out of my head. I know it sounds weird but nothing like this has ever happened to me, and what if . . .

. . . well, *what if*, at some point in your life, everyone has some sort of experience, something unusual like this, and it's supposed to mean something, to *tell* you something . . . and I just don't know what.

I mean, really, what? Don't eat seafood? What was I supposed to do, buy him? Where would I have kept him? *(Sigh)*

I mean, some people hear voices, some people have visions . . . but me, I . . . I have a spiritual experience with a . . . crab.

What the hell does that *mean*?!?

This Dream

HEIDI DECKER

(Woman, 40–50, sitting on a chair in a pool of light. The rest of the stage is in darkness. She has been sitting here for quite some time.)

WOMAN *(Impatiently, at first)*: I hate this dream. I don't know why I keep having it. It's so pointless, it doesn't make any sense. I mean, I've tried to look for hidden meaning, and there is none. None. It's just stupid.

I wish I was one of those people who is able to wake themselves up from a dream. . . . I wonder how you learn that? Hm. I thought I read somewhere that it had to do with yoga. Maybe I should take a class. . . .

I just . . . I just *hate* this part. I mean, when you're dreaming, you're stuck, there's nothing you can do. If you don't like the dream, too bad, you have to just ride it out. Just wait . . . to wake up. Or hope that somebody else will wake you up, which almost never happens when you want it to.

I'm really quite disappointed in my subconscious. I'm sure I can do *much* better than this. Everyone else has fascinating recurring nightmares . . . but . . . well just *look* at this!

I look to be at least twenty years older, in this dank little . . . house. There seems to be some evidence of children, hence the oatmeal and crayon mix stuck to the floor.

I'm always just sitting in this chair, looking out the window. Or cooking. Or scrubbing something. Or covering my face. Stupid dream. This isn't my face. My face is beautiful. Flawless.

There has *never* been a bruise on *my* face. Walking around . . . all hunched over . . . afraid of everything. I'm just . . . *in* this house. Always in this house.

Well, it doesn't matter. This dream has absolutely nothing to do with me. I just have to keep reminding myself of that . . . and soon enough I'll wake up and can let this ridiculous experience fade away in the morning sun like so much Baskerville fog.

(Very matter-of-fact) This isn't my life. My life is nothing like this . . . and I certainly do not look like this, or behave this way, or allow anyone else to . . . to . . . to treat me as if . . .

(Begins to falter a bit) . . . I'm so much *smarter* than that. I am *young*. I have dreams, I have potential. . . . I have my *whole life* ahead of me. There is so much more to *me* than this . . . *(Pause)* . . . this . . . stupid, ridiculous, dream.

I . . . I'm ready to wake up now. *(Pause)* I mean it. *(Slaps her cheek several times, lightly)*

I WANT TO WAKE UP NOW! (Pause)

Please, God, let me wake up.

Tsunami

CHRISTINA DE LANCIE

(Family mysteries, personal angst . . . can you solve your problems mathematically? Dodie, a college mathematics student, has abruptly left school and gone home to her parents. She sits alone in her old bedroom, trying to figure out an equation. As she works, she begins to hear noises and see visions. Frightened she is losing her mind, she persists in her calculations because, being a mathematician, numbers are the only way she can make sense of her world . . . which is clearly falling apart. She is convinced if she can solve The Equation she will solve her own mysterious unhappiness.)

DODIE: Right. OK.
Wittgenstein said:
"The world consists of *two* things.
Of X, and everything that is not X."
Then how the fuck do I keep coming up with . . . Y?
A *third* thing.
(She peers down at the paper.) Odd.
It would suggest:
    The whole
    is actually *greater than*
    the sum of its parts.
But that defies all the Rules of Mathematics?!
(Dodie cocks her head to one side.) I keep hearing dripping.
Anybody else? A kind of sloshing . . . No?
     So where was I? *(Draws a complete blank)*
Oh yes.
What is this *thing* that completes the whole?
. . . this Y?

(A blood curdling scream is heard coming from under the stage. Terrified, Dodie whips around.)
Is someone here?
Stand and unfold yourself!
(An Eerie Silence)
Hearing things isn't a good sign, is it?
They say that when you start hearing things, it's definitely . . . *not* a good sign.

> (Of course splitting University,
> running back home to Mommy and Daddy,
> locking yourself up in your room,
> and becoming fixated on the mathematical Grand Unifying Theory isn't *exactly* a good sign either.)

(A noose comes tumbling down from the heavens and hangs in the center of the circle. Dodie eyes it nervously.)

> I must beware the obvious.
> The Obvious is a trap for us all.

Soooo . . . *(Determined to go on)*
Not to worry! Keep it light. All is change!
(Stunned, she stops.)
Of course, mathematically, one *could* say, just as easily,
> "All is wave."

(Flashing a bewitching smile)
> Color, sound, heat, light . . . Water.

Yes, one could say, "All is Wave."
Hold on.
If *Y* is the thing that sort of transfers energy
between *X*
and everything that isn't *X*,
then . . . *Y* must be *Wave.*
Wave must be the third thing. YES!
The world consists of *three* things:
Of *X*,
everything that is not *X*,
AND WAVE.
Find the answer to the Equation of That Wave

and find the answer that explains IT ALL!
(A crumpled ball of paper falls from the heavens. Dodie picks up
the paper and reads . . .)
"There are more things in heaven and earth,
Than are dreamt of in your Philosophy, Smarty-Pants."

Per Ardua

SANDRA DEMPSEY

(It is 1942. Shirley is a forty-five-year-old farm wife whose only son, Jimmy, has been posted overseas as a Royal Canadian Air Force pilot. Shirley runs out of her house onto the porch, where the newspaper lies. She grabs the paper and rifles through it until she finds an item and scans it quickly. Once done, she is relieved, and then catches herself, suddenly aware and ashamed of what she has just done.)

SHIRLEY: I can't help myself. I know it's not right, but I have to do it. As soon as I hear the paper boy's bell, my heart stops.

Ed an' me, when I was eight months carrying Jimmy, we drove up Didsbury way—something about a horse he wanted to have a look at. That was always his favorite line. Still is. Whenever he wants to get out of the house, he always says, "I gotta go see a man about a horse."

We drove around for a couple of hours and mostly just ended up getting lost. We never did find the ranch. But by that time we were getting awful hungry, so we stopped for a bite at the Sunrise Café, on Main Street. Pretty good food—run by a nice little Chinaman and his wife. Ed had a big plate o' liver an' onions, and I remember I had a hamburger—a real treat, with bright red ketchup. It was pretty good. An' we splurged an' both had big, thick malted milks, too.

There was a fillin' station next door, and when we walked back out to our truck, Ed wandered over to have a look at a half-ton or something like that—I don't know, I can't remember exactly what. And I don't know why, but I went over to peek into a wreck that was there. I never do that sort of thing. Never.

I'll never forget it. It was sky blue, with whitewalls—a Studebaker, I think. The front was all crumpled-in pretty good, and the windshield was all gone.

For some strange reason, I went right up to it and I looked right down where the twisted steering wheel was. The seat upholstery was all torn and stained and there was glass splinters everywhere. And down on the floorboard, there was a boy's shoe wedged in between the pedals. There was dried blood all over it, and you just knew by looking at it that it was stuck in there so tight they must've had to leave it there an' pull the boy's crushed foot right out of it. He must've been in really bad shape.

I don't try to think of that wreck, that picture of the mess inside. It's not something I want to dwell on by choice. But it flashes into my mind, all the time, for no good reason—and I see that scrunched-up bloody shoe just as clear as if it was now. It's a terrible sight.

But what's worse is, every time I see it like that, in my mind, I don't think about who that poor boy might have been, or what his life might have been like, or what his mother felt when it happened. All's I can think of is, *"Thank God, it's not __my__ boy's shoe"*—as if I'm just seeing it today—an' all I am is thankful, because it's not *my* boy's shoe.

(She reopens the newspaper.) And now, every afternoon, when the paper boy throws the *Herald* onto the porch, I just have to drop what I'm doing and run to look through it. I look on every page in the first section. Some days they don't print one—sometimes, even for a few days or even a week you won't find one.

But then there it is: *"Died In Service."*

Today, it's the two-hundred-and-eightieth Official List issued by the R.C.A.F. More than seventeen hundred boys dead, or reported missing.

And I can't stop myself. I read every name. I just have to. Because that's the only way I can know my boy's alright. Pilots and navigators and gunners and bomb-aimers, I have to read

19

all those other boys' names—names I recognize, boys I've watched grow up around here.

When *their* names appear on that list, I'm *relieved.* I know I can make it to the *next list.* Because *my* boy's name isn't one of them. What kind of a mother that makes me—I don't know. I just don't know. But I do know I'll never, ever get the picture of that bloodied shoe out of my mind. And I'll never *not* be *glad* to read all those *other boys' names.*

(She tightens the paper in her fist and runs back into the house.)

Guadeloupe

MINDI DICKSTEIN

(Janie, an American tourist visiting Guadeloupe, is a formerly bored and frustrated American girl who finds her milieu and her metier in this revolutionary island world. She is seducing Virginie Tom, the lovelorn lesbian leader of the revolutionary Alliance, whose coup is falling apart.)

JANIE: I feel like I'm standing on a tall ship, with white, white sails billowing behind me. I'm floating in a harbor and you're standing on the beach, waving to me. And you're naked. And you're dropping tiny red flowers on the sand. And there are naked men and women everywhere. And I've slept with all of them: some of them don't like to fuck but do like to touch me, some of them like to whisper sexy stories in my ear and some of them like to moan and groan and some of them like me to say dirty words and some of them like me to swear that I love them, and some of them like to pretend that we're other people. Happy people. Carefree people. And nearby is a village. And there are thatched huts. And wooden canoes. And beads made from shells. And birds. And lizards. Tiny sand crabs. Rustling palms. Lapping water. Hot wind. Listen: can you hear the drums? They're calling to you. They're calling words of comfort and joy. Listen. Forget about freedom, they say. Forget about self-rule and justice. Don't clutter your head with a lot of unattainable ideals. Listen to Janie. Listen and watch and follow Janie. Janie. Janie standing on a balcony. Yes. That's it. There I am. Can you see me? I'm standing on a balcony, looking out over a crowd of happy faces, all of which are cheering me. And I'm wearing something sheer, so that people can see my body through the veils, and—oh—look at that! I am reaching down and touching myself. Yes. I'm standing there amid cheering and I am touching myself and—oh rapture! Suddenly, the Flying Nun appears. Can you see her? Sally Field flying over the crowd in her habit and she is waving at me. Waving at me! Floating through the air above the cheering masses—who all turn into large baked potatoes covered with cheddar cheese—and I am coming and the Flying Nun rises and dips over the crowd and my hand, my free hand, becomes gigantic as I reach out over the railing of the balcony into my people's mashed potato faces and I dip my fingers into them and eat them and I fly! I am just like the Flying Nun. I fly and come and eat and dip and I become gigantic and all the people bow down and worship me. All the people. All the people like you. People who need. People who want. And I know what the people want. And I know what you need. How to give it. How to take it away. Listen. Listen to the drums. Listen to what they are saying. Sex. Sex. Sex. Sex is life. Sex is love. Sex is power. Sex is revolution.

Welcome Party

ELIZABETH NELL DUBUS

(Ruth Bolton, a woman in her early sixties, is the recent widow of David Bolton, a prominent attorney and judge. Her daughter, Laura, has come to see her mother for the first time since they buried David some nine months before.)

RUTH: I wasn't crying, Laura. I was much too angry to cry. Going through all those boxes of mementos of David's career. The plaques, the honorary degrees—I looked at them, and I thought of the cost—and I got so *angry*.

I sat there and looked at that stack of paper and metal and wood, and I thought, Wonderful. Boxes of public testimonials to the brilliant lawyer, the wise judge. But for memories of our personal life? One thin scrapbook of souvenirs. *(Beat)* It's a good thing the university law center picked them up so quickly. I know I'd have made a bonfire of the whole damn lot. *(Beat)*

No one could understand why David married me, you know. I could just hear all those bright, super-achievers saying, "Now why would he marry Ruth?" One girl—she'd dated David a year—was sure he'd married me because I was pretty. But he could have chosen from hundreds of girls prettier than I. Because back then—before women started disfiguring themselves—going around looking like hobos or physical education instructors—lots of women were pretty. No, David had other reasons for marrying me. *(Beat)* For a long time, of course, I thought he married me because he loved me. I loved him, and he loved me, and we would marry and live happily ever after. Later, I realized I was wrong. That I loved him, but he didn't love me. Lord, what a sad, miserable time that was! And then later still—I stopped loving him. So then it was all right. Because by the time I did—there wasn't any him anymore. There was just—the lawyer. The judge.

And I realized—once I didn't love him anymore—that David married me because I'm—small. My life is small. A person with such a small life wouldn't demand a whole lot of room. There'd be tons of it for him—for that very large life his brilliance made. *(Beat)* For a while, I did try to have a larger life. To have achievements of my own. I loved to sew, you know. But I ruled that out right away. David hated my sewing. He thought it would make people think I had to make my own clothes. I didn't have the words to make him understand how—exciting—it was. Going into a fabric shop with an idea in my head—a picture torn from a magazine—a dress someone wore in a movie. Why, my favorite negligee on our honeymoon was one I copied from Claudette Colbert! *(Beat)* Anyway. I knew it couldn't be sewing. So then I thought of bridge, and maybe trying to be a Life Master. But to tell you the truth, I can't stand duplicate. I like to play bridge with people like—well, like *me*. And even if it does take a lot of brains to be a Life Master—that's not exactly the kind of mental effort your father admired.

I know David never thought I would win any prizes. That was his department. And, of course, yours. But can't you understand? There you were, sweeping the boards, the two of you filling the house with trophies—maybe I just wondered what it would feel like, to be one of the people whose name is called. *(Beat)* To be like you and your father—you're just like him, you know. I remember one day looking at you and thinking that listening to you was like hearing David's ideas coming out of the mouth of a very young child. It scared me to death! And then—I felt sad. Because no matter how hard I looked, I couldn't see the tiniest place where you resembled me at all.

I felt—surrounded. Two brilliant people, closing in on me. There were times when I felt absolutely—under siege. *(Beat)* I would sit there with your father at the other end of the table and you between us. And something would come up, something you were studying in school—and he'd get up and go to the library and come back with a stack of books and open them all over the table—eating with one hand, turning pages with the other—another family dinner turned into an academic tête à tête.

You don't want to hear me say I didn't love him—but it's a lot more complicated than that. And you're shocked that I stopped going out to his grave—at first, of course I did. But then the third or fourth time I'd gone out there—I put my flowers in the vase, and then I stood there—sort of *waiting*. I don't know what I was waiting for. Some kind of communion, I guess. A sense of David's presence, the kind of thing friends have told me they feel.

But I felt nothing. I stood there getting fidgety, wishing I were anywhere but there. And then—then I realized that I felt just the way I used to feel when I had to go to those *functions* with David—the ones where he made a speech or got some honor or other—and I told myself—Ruth, you have spent a great deal of your life worshipping at this man's shrine, and you do not have to do it one minute longer. So I left. And except for the day they set the marker—I never went back.

That day marked the end of a life in which for months, years, even—I was so frightened I didn't dare do anything that might call attention to me. I kept doing everything that was asked of me—I kept feeding the idol, the all-consuming image the public adored. And then, finally, I faced the biggest lie of all, the one that kept me doing this all those exhausting, terrible years. I made myself realize that *nothing* I did would be, could be, enough—but what was worse—the idol didn't even see me any more. I could be anyone. Which, of course, meant that I was—nothing.

You're going to have to get used to it, Laura. I'm not holding down the fort any more. I'm not keeping the home fires burning. For the first time in a very long time—I'm looking out for myself.

Acme Temporary Services

LINDA EISENSTEIN

(A comfortable swivel chair, bare stage. Bridge, an unconventional personnel recruiter with a machine-gun laugh, addresses an unseen applicant. Bridge is part Jewish mother, part Mafia don.)

BRIDGE: This, THIS is an impressive application. Very impressive. Solid typing test, spelling excellent, vocabulary, whew! English major, right? I can always tell.

So the work history is, let's face it, a little spotty, a few gaps here and there, but what the hell. You look like an ideal hire. In fact, why don't we admit it? You are overqualified for almost every piss-ant seat-warming job we handle.

But here at Acme Temporary Services, we are looking for special clients just like you. We search high and low for one rare qualification. It's called: a sense of reality.

So, here's the sixty-four-thousand-dollar question.

What are you looking for in a temporary agency? Do you expect that by filing this excellent resume with us—that you are eventually going to find the job of your dreams, a permanent position on an upwardly mobile career track that pays well and is meaningful and has good health insurance and a pension plan and contributes to the general weal? *(Makes a loud buzzing sound)* ANNNNH! Guess again! Of course you won't. If that's what you're looking for, take another toke on your crack pipe, go across the street to one of our competitors: Womanpower or The Pink Glove Girls, or some other lying scumsucking peddler of illusions for codependent morons. You are not for Acme and Acme is not for you.

See, at Acme we deal in reality. We know what the contemporary corporate market is looking for: warm bodies, hungry bodies, desperate bodies that will chase the carrot and bend to the stick until they drop, even though anyone with one half-blind eye can see that the days of a permanent pensioned labor force have gone the way of the dodo.

In short: temporary employees are toilet paper. Toilet paper! We know that. They know that. And at Acme, we want YOU to know that. Because if you are toilet paper, fit only to wipe the ass of the system, then you might as well be GENERIC toilet paper.

It's all summed up in our Acme philosophy: Ack Me If I Care.

See, that is the beauty in being an Acme client. When you work for Acme, you do not need to care. These bastards aren't paying you enough for you to care. If they want you to dress like you care, or pretend like you care, they should have to pay more. Just like with toilet paper. It costs extra to get the squeezably soft brand. At Acme, we don't care about your rough edges. Leave splinters in the system's hemorrhoids— Ack me if I care. For $8.50 an hour, no benefits? It's all they deserve, honey-bunny.

So. You come to work for Acme, you don't have to change a thing. Wear whatever you want. I don't care if you show up in a purple Bozo wig, miniskirt, and combat boots. You're there to type behind a fucking partition. They don't like the way you look, they can shut their eyes.

So. Are you an artist or a queer, or both? HAHAHA! No offense, it's where we advertise. Where'd you hear about us, *Variety, Art News, Advocate,* what? Hey, no sweat, you don't hafta be, Acme is an equal opportunity employer. I got Jehovah's Witnesses and Mormons over here, too—they only work on the days they're not witnessing door to door.

See, I don't care what you do in your real life. I mean, we know THIS isn't your real life, this is just the temporary cash cow, okay? We got all kinda people on our payroll. Jazz musicians, playwrights, rock and rollers, drag queens, lesbian mothers who collect for the March of Dimes, you name it. One guy, little skinny guy, he wears an octopus for a jockstrap and screams poetry in Pig Latin in junkyards. Ack me if I care!

As a matter of fact, we do have one unique benefit. Besides the fact that you don't have to put on with us, which in MY opinion is a great benefit, but hey, we're talking money now. We know that many of our clients, the ones who pass the reality check, are artists and/or misfits of one kind or another. So we established the Acme Foundation for the Arts. Acme FArts, for short. We take 10 percent of the weekly payroll, not your share, OUR mark-up—and every week we give it away to one of our employees, guaranteed.

That's right. No forms, no grant applications, no artistic statements, no peer review, no groveling, no references, no explanations that your art is relevant to the liberation of the ecosystem, no bullshit. It's a lottery! My four-year-old granddaughter throws a dart at the payroll list, every week we got a lucky winner, guaranteed. And the average payout, darling, is ten grand. Lump sum.

We can afford it. We got temps all over town, slaving away at eight, ten-fifty an hour; we gross a hundred grand a week off the toil of your collective labor. So we kick back a little. I mean, wouldn't you rather have a fighting chance at ten grand, lump sum, than an extra 85 cents an hour? Who else is gonna give you ten grand, no strings, no reports? The NEA? Hahahahaaaaaaaa!!!! Fund your next art opening, go to Rio, or stay home and rent porno movies for the next three months, I don't give a shit, it's mad money, you earned it. And you can even put "Artists Fellowship, Acme Foundation for the Arts" on your resume, earn brownie points.

See, most temporary employees don't realize it, but you have THEM by the balls. I mean, you're not TRYING to get a permanent job, and they're not going to GIVE you a permanent job, even if you wanted one, you're just the toilet paper they stuff up their crack. But if there's no toilet paper? If they're left there bare-assed in the stall, pants around their ankles, yelling for that toilet paper and no toilet paper is there? Well. Then they have to get their hands dirty. And they don't like that. No they don't. So leave 'em with their pants down often enough, they will learn to DEAL with you.

They're all out there playing HyperCapitalist hardball, thinking they're gonna grind everybody down into dirt-like clumps of anxiety. I say, join the Acme Army. Be among the people who know the score. We're in a service economy, bubbe. The multinational pirates are looting everything in sight, trying to make everybody on the bottom knife each other in the groin for a crust of stale bread.

But here at Acme? At Acme, all you have to do is show up. Show up and do your own thing. You can wear the Acme flag in your lapel, and say with absolute reality, "Ack me if I care." Because whenever you like? You're outta there.

Zombie Grrls from the Crypt

LINDA EISENSTEIN

(A Goth-style young woman. Music in the background, with
a heavy beat, might be good, too.)

Vampires
have all the fun.
They get all the good press,
all the hip attention.

Because vampires are about sex, of course. Everyone knows
    that!
Illicit sex, forbidden sex,
dangerous sex, the kind
that swoops down on you, wraps
you in its cloak and infects you against your will.
Total loss of control.
A ruby mouth at your throat. Ahhhh . . .

Yeah, right.
So why I do I have this thing
for Zombie Grrls?
It's not politically correct
to hanker after mindless rotting corpses.

Even werewolves have a better rep.
They're Jungian, at least: getting in touch with your animal
    nature,
fur, teeth, claws,
the Call of the Wild,
ahwooooo . . .

Nobody ever wrote a book called *Women Who Run with the Zombies.*
Unless you can buy it in the business section.

See, zombies are the underclass of the gothic. They're kind of like the typing pool.
Maybe that's what makes me go for that zombie grrl. Just look at her. Dirt
under her broken fingernails,
trying to claw her way out of that grave.

She's got such determination.
Stick-to-it-iveness.
There she is, six feet under, flesh turning to worms
—her eyes glazed from the nothing she stares at
all day, all week, all year.
She can barely remember she has a past,
a personality, or anyone who ever loved her.
She's been nailed in, shoved under so deep,
She's nothing but maggot food—

But even so, you can see her battered arm,
waving, trying to emerge from under the dirt.
And she's hungry. Hungry
for her stolen life.

See, a vampire is a different kind of hunger.
He's about power. He's the one who takes.
A vampire is always a top.
And there's never, ever a mark on him.

But that zombie grrl of mine:
she's got bruises and scars.
Her history is written all over her flesh.
You can see the chunks taken out of her.

At times you can see
right down to exposed bone.

Notice that shuffle? Her left leg
drags just a bit. And her hair is a wreck.
She's no fashion plate—hell, she's dead to fashion.
She's wearing whatever they buried her in.
And there's always mascara
caked under her eyes,
as though she cried herself to sleep
in her coffin.

There's no saving her.
That's what they all say.
She's a goner. No way out.
No escape from the locked limbs,
the vacancy under the lids,
there'll be no Sleeping Beauty wake-up kiss.

But I don't want to believe it.
I want to cover those cracked lips
with mine, to breathe the kiss
of life into those collapsed lungs.

I want that zombie grrl to wake up,
come back to life. But not
before she does some serious damage.

I want to see a whole zombie grrl army
march out of the crypt,
turn over desks, set cars on fire.
I want to see them turn on the hero,
advancing relentlessly,
in the face of bats, fire, shotguns, axes:
They'll keep on coming, grasping,
clutching, howling

to get their lives back,
the only ones they have.

They'll keep on coming, advancing,
willing to smash the hero
if he's stupid enough
to stand in their way,

and I yell:
GO! Go Zombie Grrls, Go!
Don't let them stop you! Oh, no . . .
GO! Go Zombie Grrls, Go!
Don't let them shut you up that way—
ever again!

Breasts

ANNIE EVANS

(Blitz is in her mid-twenties. Her hair is very short.)

BLITZ: I have to say, I have always had a very trying relationship with my breasts. Like how they sprouted just a tad in fifth grade, not much, like two water-bottle tops, but enough for Amy Duggan to whisper around the back of our station wagon that "Blitz has the biggest tits in town and everybody knows it"—that's my name—Blitz. My Dad's invention after the way I'd trounce any game board that was on the living room floor—Stratego, Life, Risk—suddenly two-year-old feet were upon them—BLITZ !!!—but we were talking about my breasts, tiny sprouts causing jealousy and fear to plague little Amy's flat-chested brain and making me feel—guilty. Because it wasn't true. Jennifer Nolan had the biggest tits that year. She came back from summer vacation and, well, started a breast fever that broke out all over the fifth grade. I wonder how she is. If premature titage had lasting damage. Boys were just . . . paralyzed by her. I'll never forget the day we were playing keep-away on the playground, boys against girls, as always, and someone threw the ball to Jennifer and it was like the game utterly stopped, because every boy on the field jumped on her. There they were—a pile of boys—all on top of Jennifer trying to cop a feel—and the rest of us girls just staring, shocked, at the power of breasts. Look what they make boys do. *(Looks at watch)* I'm a little early, aren't I? That's me, chronically early. Anyway, my little ladies took one look and said, "No way, we aren't going to be boy-pile fodder," and held up a big stop sign to my pubescent hormones. God, I hope you don't mind all this breast talk, my breast loop as my boss calls it. My boyfriend at college would always say breasts didn't matter—then I'd catch him staring at someone bursting out of her varsity sweater. "What is it!" I'd beg. He'd just shrug. How can the species that invented the peephole explain itself? My response was to start taking the pill. Amazing what happens when you develop hormonally induced tits and people start to notice—not that I suddenly had two knockers here, but enough for a groove, a plunge. My Dad, God, he noticed, but was too embarrassed to mention it. There were no visible sex organs in our house. Dad's friend Joe noticed. "I see Blitz got a visit from the tit fairy. What are they teaching you up at that expensive college, how to snag a husband?" But you know what kills me? I *was* proud. I felt more womanly. I'm looping again. Sorry. Breasts on the brain. But just to finish my story, I went off the pill because they got so goddamn tender, so they shrunk and I got pissed at them again. And pissed at myself for being pissed! Then I became militant. Started wearing those jogging bras that just strap you flat. Take that! Funny, I was finally ready to develop a healthy, working relationship with my breasts when it—when I found it. See, a few months earlier I'd met Stan. Stan my breast man. Amazing what a decent lover can do for a girl. Stan aided and abetted my revolutionary discovery that there is a direct connection from my breasts to my—well, you know. No passing go. Just—WOW, did God just install cable! He e-mailed from Australia when he heard—wanted to know if it was my left or right. "Your left has a particularly roaring fifth gear." It was my right—not my left, so I still can go into fifth. I guess. I haven't tried since—well, the right one is gone. And my right lymph nodes. For safety. Like the chemo and radiation. Up my percentage points. I still find it one of the hard things to say, that and I love you. I wish I could be more militant *now*. Yes. I had my right breast cut off. Cancer. Yes, I am so young. What the fuck of it? You think that isn't the *first* thing I said to my doctor?! You don't get breast cancer at my age! I just found out how they work, for chrissake, don't take one away!

When I came out of everything, operation-wise, the first thing I saw was my Dad, leaning on his cane, looking at my face, but not my body, like it wasn't there. "Dad, you can look, it's all bandaged, there's nothing to see." He never could look at them, at me, straight between the nipples so to speak. I remember one time, god, I was maybe fourteen, Dad wasn't looking at me, but his friend Joe was, and I know they thought I couldn't hear, but I could, and Joe let fly that maybe my brain would stop growing soon so my hormones could kick in. And Dad nodded. I just wanted . . . to die. That way you really want to die, until you're faced with real dying. My doctor, though, was Mz. Optimistic. My dying wasn't a possibility for her. We do this, and this and this and then five years from now you're free, you have a kid, get a mortgage. I was lucky in one way. I had that hospital routine down from Dad's stroke. I read, exercised, went to support groups. Same stuff I'd tried to get him to do. We'd all sit in his room, I'd read him the *Wall Street Journal*, research the best doctors, the best rehabs. The only thing I couldn't do . . . that's always been so god-damn hard . . . was saying those words. I love you. Whatever it is—I'm laced up to the neck, or I feel like I'd be giving myself away. I couldn't, so, I didn't, or if I did, it was the correct response, I didn't feel it. I just did what had to be done—and escaped. *(Looks to watch)* Geez—I thought he'd be ready for me by now. I don't know anything about tattoo parlors—how long it takes. Where do they sterilize the needles? I know it's painful but pain, ha! I never felt any cancer pain. Not a bit. Healing pain. Emotional, anger pain, fuck-you pain. God, I just want to move on! But it's never that clean, is it? Even when what you're leaving behind is a carcinogen. I chose this vine—see. *(Holds up picture of vine with grapes)* To weave around the scar—a vine, the producer of grapes, wine, song, I don't want a fake nipple—or a new breast. I don't know why I chose this instead. I don't want to forget it maybe, not that I would, me Miss Breasts-on-a-Loop, I don't know, I don't have an answer really. I guess I'll have to start dating bikers now, they'll get it, or have some insight. I won't know what to say to them. Men. Boys. I don't know the power of just one breast. I do know I wanted something else, something green. Rather then replace it, tell it finally—this is how I feel about you now. Where you were on my body. Next to this one, who's got to get through life without her twin. How I feel after all we went through growing up. After you saw that pile of boys and froze at an A cup. After I pumped you with hormones and strangled you with a jogging bra. It's like with my Dad. I couldn't say it for so long—and I finally did. When I was going in. With connection. He was crying— he always cries now that he's had his stroke. Hymns, road kill. It's so embarrassing for Mom—and me. Anyway, I'm going up to surgery, and I turn and see him there with his cane, so frail, like a lost child, a child who'd been where I was going, and it just flowed out like a clear, clean stream. I love you, Dad. It felt good. Really good. And I thought, great, it'll be easy from now on. Well, I was wrong, it's not. But I know I did it once with grace. And now, with grace, I'm telling her *(Looks down)*, telling you. I love you. And I miss you. And with this bit of green and grapes, I'll be able to keep doing it, even if the neck laces tighten and it gets hard again. And I'll be able to tell my lover, show him, whoever he will be, and my kid, and my mortgage broker—see—bounty.

Parmachene Belle

CAROLYN GAGE

(Cornelia "Fly Rod" Crosby, a tall transgender woman, 42, sits upright in a hospital bed. She holds a split bamboo fly rod and is practicing casting—ideally out over the heads of the audience. Dressed in a hospital gown, she wears a battered felt hat, with hand-tied flies in the hatband. It's January 1899. After a moment she reels in.)

CORNELIA: Not hittin' too good today, are they? Ayuh. Let's see what we got on here . . . *(She examines the leader.)* Ayuh. Got a brown hackle on the end of the tippet and a dragonfly on the dropper. Well, that tells the story plain enough . . . Imitations. Got nothing but imitation flies on here. *(Looking up)* Know what an imitation is, don't you? Something that's trying to look like something that it's not. Now, let's see . . . *(She takes her hat off and examines the flies on the band. After a moment, she selects one.)* I think this is what the doctor ordered. *(She holds it up.)* The Parmachene [pronounced "parma-*chee*-nee"] Belle. Ayuh. The Parmachene Belle. *(She begins to remove the brown hackle.)* I've been a Maine huntin' guide for almost twenty years, and there aren't many flies I haven't seen. Royal Coachman, Professor, Scarlet Ibis, Grizzly King, Queen of the Waters . . . I've used 'em all . . . But if I had to do with just one fly, it would be the Parmachene Belle. Caught two hundred trout in one day at Kennebago with this little beauty. *(Holding up the Parmachene Belle)* See that bit of red feather there? You won't find a single insect in the great state of Maine looks like that. Nope. Not a livin' creature— wet or dry—looks like the Parmachene Belle, except the Parmachene Belle. She doesn't imitate anything but herself.

And that's why they call her a "fancy." *(Attaching the Parmachene Belle to the tippet)* Don't get me wrong. I use the imitations, too. I just don't swear by them the way some folks do. There's anglers I've met who think that all you have to do is figure out exactly what the fish are eatin', what time of year, what part of the river, what time of day—and what fork they're usin' to eat it with—and there's your fish. Fly-fishin' is an exact science, accordin' to them. They don't have much patience with the fancies like the Parma Belle—or the few who use 'em. *(She takes off her hat.)*

Had a sporter come up here from Boston one time. That's what we call the summer folks who hire the guides—"sporters." Fellow was a lawyer. Ayuh. A Boston lawyer. *(Pausing to put the brown hackle back in the hatband)* Well, this pen-pusher fellow had been studyin' up on brook trout. Figure he knew more about the trout than they knew about themselves. Tied his own flies, too. Ayuh. Must have had about a hundred—and every one an imitation. Not a single fancy in the lot. *(Looking at the hackle on the hatband)* Everything had to look like something or it wasn't anything. *(Replacing the hat on her head, she takes up the rod again.)* Master smart fly-tier, too. Had himself flies made with joints, so they'd waggle in the water. Used big fish scales for the wings on his midge fly and his grasshopper. Looked just like the real thing. Even had a mayfly that would float. Carved it out of cork. Master smart tier. *(She casts the Parma Belle.)*

So me and this Boston pen pusher we're out on Cupsuptic Lake in my canoe. It's late in the afternoon, about four, and the water's so calm it looks like a sheet of glass. We've been out about two hours without so much as a rise, when suddenly the water starts dimplin' up in front of us. Trout were comin' up to feed. And pretty soon that water is just boilin' with 'em. So the sporter starts castin', and I don't mind tellin' you that little pen pusher could lay one of the prettiest casts I've ever seen—right over the boil, and do it again and again. But, nothing. Whatever he was sellin', those trout just weren't in the mood to buy. So he starts fumdiddlin' with his flybook, huntin' around for one of his imitation doo-jigs. "Match the hatch," as they say. Well, by this time, the trout are startin' to sink, so I take out my rod. Pen-pusher fellow sees this and he gets himself all humped up like a hog goin' to war. Just what kind of fly do I think is going to do a better job than his hand-tied, custom-deluxe, fish-scale, cork-body, wiggle-waggle imitations? So I show him the Parma Belle—like I just showed you. Well, that little red feather was like a matador's cape to a bull. He takes one look and he's *off*. *(She imitates him.)* "What's *that* supposed to be?" And I say, "A Parmachene Belle." And he says, "But what's it *supposed* to be?" And I look at him, calm as a clock, and I say, "A Parmachene Belle." Well, his face is lookin' like a starched shirt. He's come all the way down from Boston with a flybook full of imitations of every creature that ever crawled or hatched its way off of Noah's Ark, and here's this jillpoke of a huntin' guide from East Overshoe—and a *lady* guide at that— and he's payin' her his good money to go fishin' with a fly that doesn't look like anything God ever put on this earth. And if that's not enough to make Napoleon cry, it's a fly with a red feather in it! Well, that Boston lawyer, he just starts plasterin' it all over the wall about folks from the State of Maine in general and about ladies from the State of Maine in particular—and he's tellin' me how it's just like a woman to be gettin' all notional about the fancies—pickin' out her flies the way she would be pickin' out a hat. But to tell you the truth, I don't remember too much of what he said after that, because just then a twelve-inch lunker smashed the Parma Belle clear to the gills, and after that, I had my hands full just keepin' her on the line. Well, the pen pusher durn near tips over the bark, grab-bin' for his rod, and he's starts whippin' the water some fierce. Meantime, I'm yankin' 'em out of the water, one right after the other, and sometimes two at a time! By the time the sun went down, I had me the prettiest gad of trout you ever laid your eyes on. Ayuh. Boston fellow never got a single strike. Skunked. Ayuh. You can believe he was singing pretty small on the way back to camp. But I told him not to feel too bad about it, because the trout that took the Parma Belle were probably all females anyway—out shoppin' for hats when they should have had their mind on feedin'.

I guess you could say I'm kind of a Parmachene Belle myself. Six feet tall and a huntin' guide. Not too many other gals like me. None, in fact. But I get the strikes. Ayuh. Everything hits the Parma Belle. Of course, you don't want to keep everything that hits—just the ones that are sportin'. That's why, when the men come courtin', I always toss 'em back. They'll hit anything. Too much like landing chub. *(She laughs and becomes serious.)* Women—they're the keepers. *(She jerks the line.)* See that! Had a hit there!

In the House of the Moles

TERRY GALLOWAY

[Wark's mother, Peg, has just died. Wark (a Scottish word for both "work" and "misery") hovers over her mother's body, looking jittery and lost.]

WARK: I never did think it could happen to her. Not Peg. I always thought if death ever tried to get the jump on Peg she'd just turn around and whack its rear. *(Short laugh)* But here she is. I wish I could feel a little sorrier about it. It's not like I didn't love her. I did. I mean, she was our mama. But I don't know. I just don't feel like crying or nothing. Not the way I did when my little sweetie died. He was the best little cat that cat. Real dainty. Lots of fluff on his paws. When he didn't want me talking he'd put his paws on my lips patpatpat. Real sweet. No one else ever told me shut up that sweet. Why something had to happen to a smart little cat like that I don't know, but it did. He was hung up on that wire no way he could move. I said, "kitty kitty kitty" and he kind of meowed, just making the motion, not hardly a sound. And then he died. I picked him up to hold him and then he died. He lived for a minute and then he died. I knew it when it happened 'cause when the heat left his body it went into mine. It ruined my dress. But I'm glad I was there. I'm glad it was me there holding him when he died and I was the last sure thing he felt. *(She looks about to weep.)* Ah, hell. I hate it she died alone like that.

Sweetie's Not

ELIZABETH GILBERT

(Thea, in her forties, is driving her younger sister Olive to east Texas for their parents' surprise sixtieth wedding anniversary party. John Leonard, Olive's husband of twenty years, has just run off with a woman in her twenties.)

THEA: The one good thing about being married, Olive, is you don't have to worry about being found dead by strangers. It happens. It happens a lot. Just watch the news. Having everything you'd kept hidden for so long just all splayed out there. Awful. 'Cause there's never an absence of audience. No matter what people are in the middle of doing, they'll stop for a chance to see a stinking, decomposing body. They could be in the middle of a haircut, sucking down margaritas, or whatever. They'll come on over. *(Beat)* But, that's not gonna happen to you, Olive. And you know why? 'Cause long before anyone gets to wondering about what the hell that smell is creeping out from under your front door, your husband, and you will have a husband, even if it's not John Leonard, your husband's gonna find you. That's right. He'll be reading the morning paper, or letting out the cats, or getting ready to take his morning dump, and he'll have to go to wondering. You know, I haven't seen my Olive around lately. Where the hell is she? *(Reaches over to pat Olive on the knee)* Never succumb to passive acceptance. Say that, Olive. Good. I will not be unhappy. I actively seek alternatives. I actively seek alternatives. That's right. Solutions are always possible. C'mon. Say it. I will not be unhappy. For Christ's sake, Olive. Just say it. It works. Caroline down at the florist did it and it completely changed her life. And it was in more of a ruin than yours, believe you me. I will not be unhappy.

Islands of Civility

MAGDALENA GOMEZ

(A 1950s elementary school classroom in New York City. The Patient, a forty-nine-year-old Latina, sits beneath a student desk. An American flag engulfs the space, and a clock is stopped at noon. The Patient is addressing her therapist. The classroom is in her memory and represents how she is feeling in this moment of equal vulnerability and strength. The Patient feels herself within her childlike body as she retraces a path of memories.)

PATIENT: I was born four months after the Rosenbergs were executed.

I remember school air raid drills. A single peep would make me responsible for the deaths of all my classmates. I would be silent for my country. I was five years old.

Later that same year, I was sodomized by someone called an uncle, warned that my mother would be turned over to the Russians if I told. I crossed my heart with religious silence. I thought all Russians were mean, pudgy, bald white guys who spit when they talked. I didn't know there were Russian women and children.

In seventh grade, I refused to wear a white shirt and red tie to the school assembly where I refused to salute the flag. I knew a pledge was a promise. My mother and father had taught me that a promise is a serious thing. They taught me that your word was your honor and that when you're poor your honor is all you have. I didn't know what "Allegiance" meant; I tried to look it up, but I couldn't spell it.

As for the shirt and tie, I didn't think that anybody, except maybe my mother, should be telling me how to dress.

The most important thing was the promise. At one assembly, our chorus teacher, Mrs. Payne, forced my hand to my chest. I walked out. The principal couldn't find me anywhere after that. I hid in a closet till the school day was over. Later, my friends told me that he had called me a stinking little communist with all the hairs in his nose standing at attention.

I told my mother. She didn't speak English or read or write in any language. I didn't know what a communist was, and Mami didn't really know either. As it turns out, even people who knew how to read only knew what they saw in the movies. I told her about the Pledge thing and she said I was right. She asked my forgiveness for being an ignorant woman but that she was sure of one thing: only God deserved blind faith.

The next day she went with me to school and told the principal, in his own office, in front of a desk the size of Brooklyn, that first of all, nobody was going to tell her daughter how to dress, this was America, after all. And most important, she said, that no decent person should make a promise they don't understand. She admitted she'd never gone to school, but it seemed like common sense to her that children deserve explanations. She asked him, Mr. Peck, that was his name . . . come to think of it, I think every teacher's name in that school started with a "P" . . . she asked him why no one had taught me what the Pledge meant; with heat from his liver rising, he mumbled that good children must do as they are told. My mother softly told him she was raising a daughter, not a sheep. I was translating back and forth but left out the part when he said that my mother was a stupid woman and it was people like her who were destroying America. I told him he better take it back or I would tell my father, and my father was nobody to mess with. The school bell rang and he snorted so deep it was like he'd kicked up a lot of mucous that had probably sat caked in his nose for decades. He lunged for the tissue box and took it with him as he slammed the door. Mami stared at his empty desk for a moment, and smiled, just

45

a little. She squeezed my hand and asked if I'd like to take the long way home.

Till this day I keep my heart uncovered. I avoid baseball games all together. Someday I hope to see liberty and justice for all. My mother and father said I should work for it and meanwhile, never make a promise I didn't understand. I wish I'd learned that sooner. I thank my mother, I thank my father. They didn't raise no sheep.

Queer Fruit

SARA HARDY

(Eddy, a "mature age" ex-performer, jovial. Born around 1910, she's lived through "interesting times" and has now reached the 1970s—enjoying the liberated "second wave" of feminism. She is well seasoned, loves show business, and has a good sense of humor, especially about herself.)

EDDY: I tell you—that first time, thrust into bed with the woman I loved! I didn't know where to put myself! Course I knew there was *something* going on between us. I mean you know, don't you—something . . . zingy, going on. But then, I *didn't* know, you know, what exactly it was. Because you see we had no role models, no examples, you didn't see it in the streets like you do now. All you had was *The Well of Loneliness* to go on. I cried at the end of that book, I cried and cried. Poor Stephen (she was the main character)—Poor Stephen, I thought, that's me, that is *me*. But I cried with relief, too, to *find* that book—even if I did have to cover it with a brown paper wrapper! You did you know, that book was banned as obscene when it first came out. Not the sort of thing to be caught reading on the bus! It's out of fashion now but it saved a lot of lives that book. . . . At least you knew you were *something*, not the-only-one-in-the-world—because we did, we thought that. *(Mock melodrama)* Each one in her "well of loneliness." .

Anyway, so there I was, in bed with Lydia, middle of the . war, you know, "do or die" mentality, and I thought—*do* something Eddy, *do* something! But I didn't have a clue, did I! I mean, it doesn't *say* what you do in *The Well of Loneliness*, does it. They kiss I think—yes, on the mouth, I'm pretty sure there was one of those. . . . Worth a read—*Radclyffe Hall*—bit of lesbian history after all. (But thank heaven for *RubyFruit Jungle!*)

I was certain there was *something,* you know, between us. But you can't be *sure* can you, I mean your imagination lets rip and you fantasize so much you think suddenly—this is crazy, I've made it all up, this woman simply *likes* me!

Friendship, it's a wonderful thing. However much you're in love you don't want to ruin that, do you. These days it's different, people don't get quite so shocked, do they. If you play your cards right, you can hang on to the friendship—and if you can't, well it wasn't worth having in the first place! But those days: make the *wrong move* with a woman—you'd be made an outcast, or worse.

You were so oppressed, locked in, silent . . .

I suppose all that was going through my mind—that and trying not to sweat! She kept making all these silly jokes, 'cause she was very funny, and I tried to laugh but my face was so tight I thought I had lockjaw! She was lovely, lovely, chatting away there, laughing, giggling, bouncing up and down in the bed—all "girls together having fun" sort of thing. And then I thought, if I stretch my arm out, you know, casually across her pillow . . .

We weren't naked! Never naked. We had neck-to-toe nighties, buttons tight to the collar and cuffs. You got *dressed* to go to bed in my day—especially if it was with someone else!

Anyway, Lydia's sitting up in bed doing her impersonation of Ethel Smyth conducting an orchestra with a toothbrush, and I think, "Now or never," so I casually slide my arm out across her pillow and sort of lie there you know, looking a right fool! Anyway, Lydia conducts the grande finale, and she's in quite a lather 'cause she impersonates all the instruments as well, see, and suddenly she throws her toothbrush in the air and gracefully falls back, perfectly, into my one arm embrace. And before I could say the immortal words "fancy a cuddle?"

she sort of rolled close in towards me, and kissed me, on the mouth. She was kissing me, and I was kissing her, and it was everything, all at once, hands, mouths, arms, legs, lips, everywhere, all over, hectic, urgent, passionate—a rummaging mass of whirl—a frenzy! It was wonderful! We didn't know what we were doing, but by heaven, we did it!

Bed full of buttons in the morning.

Last May, last May was when she died. I've left a space for my name on her stone—"In Love, United"—that's what I'm having. Sounds like a football team but I don't care. Best years of my life. Great happiness like that, there aren't words . . .

Joan of Arc

LAURA HARRINGTON

(The year is 1429. The scene is Joan of Arc's prison cell in
Rouen. Lady Anna is one of two noblewomen sent to examine
the seventeen-year-old Joan of Arc to prove whether or not
she is a virgin. The church and the court have ordered this
examination. Lady Anna leaves Joan's prison cell, shaken.)

LADY ANNA: The touch of her skin shocked me.
I had never before touched another woman.
Animal heat. The smell of wheat.
We touched her. Two strange women.
She opened to us. Shy. Still. Silent.
I touch her thigh,
smell the blood the Duchess has spilled breaking her hymen.
A maid. And yet a maid no more.
A girl who has never been touched.
And I am touching her.
A girl who will never be touched.
And I am touching her.
No man has ever looked at me the way I am looking at her.
She bore it. Tolerated it.
Like a horse in a barn she stood dreaming of fields and
    freedom.
Noble. Too noble to protest.
I think of the blood on her thigh,
so red, so white.
I feel her breath.
A quick intake as I place my hand on her thigh.
Will I hurt her as the Duchess has?
Break her to prove her unbroken?

The guard must look, must see.
Father Martin. He cannot lift his head.
Shame like a yoke bends his neck.
But he must write and sign his name.
Give testimony.
Each of us. A sense of shame.
Defiled in the face of her purity.
Each of us. Guilty of the rape of the maid.
A virgin has been sacrificed on the altar of the church.
We are pagans still.
And in her purity she bears it.
Eyes open. She sees. She watches. She knows.
She bears it.

Loving Enemies III

BARBARA HOMANS

(Mother is about to be put in a nursing home by her two daughters. She wears a pink nightgown, and the father's picture is on a bedside table. There is a bureau with a mirror.)

MOTHER *(Addressing the picture)*: Isaac, isn't this a pretty kettle of fish. We used to go out for breakfast, rain or shine, or else set the table at home—oatmeal, orange juice, toast burnt, buttered to the edges, cut in fours. Don't think I didn't earn my keep, twenty-four hours a day, seven days a week. Well, sweetie pie, those days are gone forever. *(Gets up slowly and goes to the window)* I've always been a woman sensitive to pain. Too much cold, too much heat. If my tooth hurts, my tooth hurts. Considering the ills the flesh is heir to, I guess I've had my fair share, childbirth, menopause—sent me to the doctors for that one. Anything, Isaac said, to get a little peace of mind. Isaac was always one for peace of mind. I must have been impossible but nothing seemed to go right. No one seemed to care. "What in God's name is going on with you?" he asked. "There must be a pill. There's got to be a pill to quiet you." And there was a pill to quiet me. I sat in the corner and knitted sweaters. I knitted then. Can't now. Arthritis. Look at these hands. God, to look at them, so bent. The rings don't fit.

Gall bladder, hysterectomy. They thought why not. There I was. Why not? I haven't lent myself to them since. Old women. They'll chop you up. It pays, doesn't it? Haven't lent myself to them since, except for the usual—blood pressure, palpitations, a woman of my age getting a little hard of hearing and can't see as well but well enough. My legs a little unsteady. *(Mother stretches a little, a very little.)* That's from lack of exercise. "You should walk two miles a day," she says, "One mile up and one mile back." Ye gods and little fishhooks, a woman of my age shouldn't walk farther than to the door if she doesn't feel like it. Not that I didn't walk enough after the last stroke, waiting on him hand and foot, seven days a week, twenty-four hours a day.

(She walks over to the dresser and she looks in the mirror.) God, Daisy Warren, you're a mess, flesh hanging from your bones, spots on your hands, but at eighty nobody's Hedy Lamarr. Wear long sleeves. It doesn't show. Did he care? Of course he cared. Wasn't blind then. Lord what a dancer he was. The handsomest man in the room. All the women doted on him. That Martha Brown. Well, she's buried now, fluttering all around him like a fool, a moth around a light. Didn't think I deserved him. Deserved him! Hand and foot I deserved him! I earned him!

(Turns) The kettle's on. I can hear it sing. I'm not deaf at all. I hear it singing but it's too early to get up. I can't remember a day when I could relax, lie back, when I didn't have a task. "The glass is always half empty for you," he said. It's pitiful. Pitiful. And then he would get up and do the things that weren't a task at all, cards, golf—"challenges," he called them. For me there were chores. *(Listens)* He'll be wanting her to get his breakfast tea, then his oatmeal—instant, no milk, raisins—orange juice, two pieces burnt cut in fours buttered to the edges. "You've skimped, Daisy." "Get it yourself you old man." No I never said that once, not in all those years. He never washed out a pan in his life. Trying to sit down to have my breakfast, "Get me my water, are these my pills, another cup of coffee sweetie pie." Clear the table, fill the dishwasher. Five thousand times. I counted that once.

I can hear him now stumbling to the bathroom. What full bladders they have, at night watching, waiting, "Get up, get up old man, the urinal's by the bed. Don't mess the carpets again." *(Starts to weep)* I'm getting too old myself, and I need you and I miss you, Isaac, and they want to put me away like an old shoe.

Sprat

DAPHNE R. HULL

[Sprat, a nondescript adult, wears solid ward clothing, is cheerful and upbeat but NOT peppy. Elven or spritely, perhaps. An eight-foot-high one-dimensional pyramid (triangle) of paper cups sits upstage; 192 cups across the bottom, 192 high. There are 200–300 cups scattered loosely about the stage around Sprat, who is cheerfully stacking a second pyramid downstage. The large pyramid may be glued together to prevent disaster and embarrassment. Sprat is most enthusiastic when counting or discussing cups. The expression "Sprat!" is equivalent in context to a profane exclamation.]

SPRAT *(Kneeling, stacking, facing audience)*: . . . 42, 43, 44, 45 . . . *(Gathers a few more cups and returns to downstage pyramid)* . . . 46, 47, 48 . . . 49 . . . 50, 51 *(Gathers, returns)* . . . 52, 53, 54, 55, 56 . . . fifty– . . . 57! *(Gathers, returns)* . . . 58, 59— OOPS! *(Knocks pyramid over)* SPRAT! Splat! *(Mutters)* Every SINGLE time . . . get too excited . . . *(Begins stacking again.)* ONE, 2, 3, 4 . . . *(Notices audience)* . . . 5 . . . OH! *(Pause)* I didn't realize anyone was here. *(Pause)* Another observation team, eh? *(Pause)* I REALLY wish they would warn me ahead of time and let me know I would be receiving guests. Hm. Oh, but you're supposedly observing me in my NATURAL habitat—am I right? Whee! Right, that's right. *(Pause)* They say they keep meaning to put in a new window for me, where you can see me, but I can't see you, you know what I mean? But, they said their budget is tight, so we will have to be satisfied with us seeing each other for now, I suppose. *(Pause, uncertain)* Well. *(Beat)* Let's see. I suppose . . . me standing here observing YOU observing ME isn't going to tell YOU much of anything . . . hmmm. Shall I . . . sing? *(Clears throat dramatically)* Fa lala la llla la laaa . . . how was that? Ahem. Mi mi mi mi mi miiiiiii—*(Cracks last high note)* Hrrrumph! *(Pause)* Ha ha ha! I don't suppose you REALLY wanted me to sing, now did you? And I CAN'T dance, soooo . . . I suppose I'll just have to be myself, won't I? It's about all I've got. Well, then. I hope you don't mind— *(Kneels)* but I'm going to work on my pyramid while you're watching. It's rather a hobby of mine. Let me see . . . *(Counts cups already stacked rapidly)* 1 2 3 4 5 *(Stacks)* 6, 7, 8, 9, 10 . . . *(Gathers, returns)* 11, 12, 13, 14 . . . 15 . . . 16 . . . 17, 18, 19, 20 . . . you know! I built THAT one back there. The big one. THAT one. One hundred and ninety-two across, one hundred and ninety-two high. All together, that makes eighteen thousand three hundred and forty cups. That's a LOT of cups! *(Muses)* They even brought a ladder in for me so I could reach the upper rows, to get it finished. But—! Only with staff supervision, of course! They were really pretty nice about it. *(Stacking)* Now, where was I . . . oh, yes! Twenty. Twenty-one, 22, 23, 24, 25 26 . . . 27 . . . *(Gathers)* 30, 31, *(Singsong)* 32, 33, 34, 35, 36, 37, 38, 39, 40, 41, 42, 43, 44 . . . *(Sly)* I'll bet you're wondering just where I got all of these cups, aren't you? Well . . . perhaps I'll tell you . . . maybe. *(Beat)* Yes, I think I will! You see, at first, I just collected them, slowly. A few each day. It was taking SUCH a long time to collect them, I wasn't able to build much of a pyramid at all! I wasn't having very much fun. Then, the doctors decided I was HOARDING, and they decided to give me ALL the cups I asked for, and gave me cups even when I didn't ask! Wasn't that just SO thoughtful of them? I think they thought I would get tired of building my pyramids. Silly them! They said something, I think, about "flooding my compulsion in an effort to dissuade me," or something along those lines. Now just LOOK at how high my pyramids are growing! The ceiling in THIS room is SO much higher than my ceiling at home, let me tell you! It allows me a much increased degree of creative freedom. *(Stacking and*

gathering continues as is indicated by counting) 45, 46, 47, 48
. . . 49 . . . *(Knocks over pyramid)* SPRAT! Splat! ONE, 2, 3, 4,
5, 6 . . . I was born on a battleground . . . 7, 8, 9, 10, 11 . . .
on the battleground. Right smack dab in the middle of everything. One on one side of me, the other on the other side of
me . . . 12, 13 . . . the fighting was fierce and hostile for quite
a little while, and it was AWFULLY loud 14 . . . sometimes so
loud I just couldn't think. Fifteen, 16, 17, 18, 19, 20, 21, 22
. . . then the Cold War began . . . which, as you can see, I sur-
vived. Twenty-three, 24, 25 . . . they stayed together for THIS
sake, and for THAT sake, and I said, for GOODNESS sake,
don't do ME any favors! Twenty-six, 27, 28, 29 . . . oops!
SPRAT! Splat! Hee hee! ONE, 2, 3, 4, 5, 6, 7, 8, 9, 10, 11,
12, 13, 14 . . . 15, 16, 17 . . . 18 . . . 19 . . . 20 . . . 21 . . .
eventually, I went AWOL in order to avoid choosing sides.
They just kept saying, What to do? What to do? And *I*
couldn't help them, after all, so I moved out and got a job.
Twenty-two, 23, 24, 25, 26, 27 . . . *(Carefully)* . . . 28 29 . . .
30! Ha! Thirty-one, 32, 33 . . . on the assembly line at THE
place to get a job in town . . . union, you know . . . 34, 35,
36, 37 . . . 38 . . . 39 . . . FORTY! Ha! Forty-one, 42, 43, 44
. . . and then I took up this hobby of mine. Forty-five, 46, 47,
48 . . . 49 . . . 50! Whee! Ha! Fifty-one, 52 . . . and it got to be
so gosh-darn LOUD at work, what with the machinery clang-
ing and banging and clicking and whirring, day in, day out;
day in, day out . . . 53, 54, 55, 56 57 58 59 . . . 60! Sixty!
Well! Sixty-one, 62, 63, 64 . . . and my pyramids began to
grow REALLY tall, I mean really tall, or at least as tall as they
COULD be, in my apartment. The ceilings here are much,
much higher. Allows far greater creative freedom. Sixty-five,
66, 67, 68, 69 . . . 70! Ha! WHO wants to spend their days
watching machinery whirr and click day in and day out, when
one COULD be building these lavish and wonderful pyramids, or SOMETHING, anyway? Really. Seventy-two, 73,
74, 75, 76 . . . I carry my dreams in a dixie cup. Seventy-
seven, 78, 79 . . . 80! They began to wonder what happened

to me. They came looking for me, eventually. They found me, building my pyramids . . . 81, 82, 83, 84, 85 . . . and they wanted to know why I spent my days building with these dixie cups! Where's yours, I asked them—but they wanted to know why I don't put water in my dixie cups instead of using them to build pyramids. And *I* said, because I carry my DREAMS in dixie cups—and that would drown them! Well, they said, WE don't see any dreams in these dixie cups. And I said, YOU don't NEED to see them; only I need to see them. Well, you can imagine . . . 86 . . . I wound up in here, because they were simply shocked when they saw all those pyramids in my apartment, and THEN to not see these dreams on top of that—well, that was just TOO much for them! *I* am proud to say that *I* had 15,672 cups in my apartment! Eighty-seven . . . 88 . . . 89 . . . but NOW . . . now I have 18,340 cups in THAT pyramid alone! I wonder what THEY would think of THAT? Ninety, 91, 92—OOPS! SPRAT! Splat! *(Gathers and resumes stacking)* ONE, 2, 3, 4, 5, 6, 7, 8, 9, 10, 11, 12 . . . *(Sings to the tune of "Here We Go 'Round the Mulberry Bush"; lights fade during song.)* I carry my dreams in a dixie cup, a dixie cup, a dixie cup; I carry my dreams in a dixie cup, so early in the morning . . . I carry my dreams in a dixie cup, a dixie cup, a dixie cup; I carry my dreams in a dixie cup, so early in the morning . . . *(Lights out.)*

Summer in the City

BARBARA KAHN

(Woman enters, looks around, sees audience, and decides to speak to them. She is obviously distraught and becomes more so as she continues to speak.)

Can I tell you a secret? I need to tell someone and there's no one else. But promise you won't tell anyone, it's really important. If certain people find out, it could ruin me in the community and with my family. Oh, God! I've been carrying this around for so long now. I feel like a phony, an impostor. I have to tell someone soon, or I'll go crazy, and then I'll really need a shrink. Oh, dear. I didn't mean to tell you like that, it just came out. That's right. I'm not in therapy. I've never been in therapy. I lied to everyone. But what was I supposed to do? I moved to New York, and I met so many nice people, and they never asked me, "Are you in therapy?" If they had, I would have said no. I would. But they all talked about how, "Therapy has turned my life around." Or, "I finally see the negative patterns in my life." Or sometimes it was, "My therapist says we shouldn't discard all of Freud—some of his insights are profound." Or else it was, "I've made so much more progress since I switched to group." And inevitably someone would turn to me and ask, "Who's *your* therapist?" And I would panic. I mean, how could I tell them that I don't need therapy—that I love my job, I'm financially secure, I adore my family, I like people but I like myself, too, so I'm sometimes alone, but I'm never lonely? It would have sounded so patronizing, so self-righteous. So I lied. I said, "Oh, I go to a therapist out in New Jersey where my family lives." After that, it got worse. They asked me things like, "Is your therapist gestalt or Jungian or what?" And I had to say, "Oh, she doesn't like labels, she takes the best from all the various disciplines." I couldn't take it. So I went to visit my family last weekend. I thought I would talk the situation over with my mom—we get along really great. Well, I no sooner arrived and told my mother I needed to have a talk, when she turned to me and said, "Sweetheart, I'm glad you brought that up. I found a wonderful support group for mothers of adult daughters. The therapist who runs it is incredible. She said that our daughters are just that—daughters. Where is it written that they have to be our best friends, too? What a breakthrough for me—I mean us, darling. I'm so sorry for all the pressure I put on you to be my friend. From now on, I don't want you to confide in me or feel like you have to share everything in your life with me. I think you should find a good therapist to help you cope with the residual effects of the undue burden I forced on you for so long." I couldn't listen anymore. Again, I lied. "Ma!" I screamed, "I'm already in therapy." And she started crying, with this big smile on her face, and said, "Baby, I'm so proud of you." So, here I am. Back in New York. It's the middle of August. And I have to pretend not only that I'm in therapy, but that I'm climbing the walls until Labor Day like everybody else, because my therapist is on vacation. Shit. It isn't fair. Even when life is great, it sucks.

That's Another Story, Dot Com

JUDY KOROTKIN

(A middle-aged woman, Sandra, is seated in a chair, facing the audience. Next to her is a telephone on a table and perhaps a computer. She is, give or take a few years, in her mid-fifties to early sixties, a motherly type, with a comic flare. She looks at the computer, shakes her head glumly and turns to the audience.)

I'm not crazy about growing older. Aside from the fact that your children think they know more than you know, and are too busy to visit on Sunday, even though they *know* you're alone, I can't stand not understanding this new world that my three kids take for granted—Rock and Rap; fat-free this and low-fat that; computer virus this and Internet that. It's really too much. I always figured that growing older meant growing smarter, wiser. But everyday I look around me and I know less and less, and it's beginning to bug me.

Take, for example, "Blah, Blah, Blah, Dot Com." Turn on the television. You watch the news, or an ad, and there it is. "For more information, contact us on Blah, Blah, Blah Dot Com." No more "Call us at Blah, Blah, Blah." Or "Drop us your question at Blah, Blah, Blah" and the address. No more of *that*. If you can't plug into "Blah, Blah, Blah, Dot Com," you're out of luck, out of the loop, old hat. You're no longer in, you're on your way out, and who needs to feel that way?

So, obviously, if I wanted to know all about Dot Com, I needed to know how to work a computer. And if you want to work the computer you have a problem if you don't *have* a computer. The time had come. I wanted a computer, I needed a computer. I wanted to connect up with the Internet, whatever that is. I wanted to browse, I wanted to send an email, whatever that was. I wanted to be up-to-date, current, with it, on the ball.

So, I started on Debby. Debby's my oldest daughter. (My younger daughter, Ellen, can't be reached during the day, and my son, Michael, lives in Washington.) Debby's husband, Pete, had been talking about buying a new computer and I wanted to make sure he didn't give the old one to anyone but me.

So my job was to let them both know how much I needed it. There's no point in my going into how I handled my Computer Campaign. That's another story. But Debby managed to convince Pete that he should give his old computer to me when he bought the new one. (By the time she got through with him, he thought it was *his* idea.)

He didn't buy a new computer right away. It was a whole drama. He shopped around, he checked the ads, he surfed the Net, whatever that means, and finally, a few months later, he announced he had bought a computer and he would deliver his old one to me, along with a new, updated Windows program. I was so excited, I could spit. I was about to dive into the computer world. The door was swinging open.

I was ready. I was willing.

But I wasn't able.

There were just too many choices: File, Edit, View, Format, Window, HELP! Just give me the old days, when you typed away on your Smith Corona with no smart-ass computer telling you that you'd misspelled a word. I had been so looking forward to the new computer world and Blah, Blah, Blah, Dot Com. But I had never expected that just learning what to do with the mouse would scare the hell out of me.

First of all, I've always hated mice, and here I had to depend on one to get anywhere. And the only windows I'd ever dealt with used Windex. I'd be typing away and suddenly

I was in another window. Whatever happened to the one I was in? So, I called Pete at the office to ask him how I got back my window.

How should I know I interrupted him at a meeting? I guess that's why he was so cranky.

"Look, Sandra," (He made a point of calling me by my first name; "Mom" was something he reserved for his mother) "either minimize it or close out the window."

"How?" I asked.

"Look," he said. "I'm in the middle of a meeting. Call me at home tonight. Just hit the Start icon and get out of it. It will save itself. And look—read the manual. I told you to read the manual." He hung up.

I sat staring at the computer screen. Why would I hit Start to turn off the computer? Ridiculous. And what was even more ridiculous was that I was scared.

What was I scared of? Okay. I hit Start, even though I thought that made no sense at all. And suddenly the damn computer threw a box on the screen that frightened the hell out of me. It gave me a choice. Programs, documents, help, accessories, etc. Oh, there it was: "Shut down." But the mouse wouldn't cooperate. I don't know how it happened, but I was suddenly in Window 2. How the hell do I get out of this? I was terrified.

Maybe I broke it! Well, I couldn't call Pete at work, so I called Debby at work. She, too, was in the middle of something. Well, it was obvious that I would have to call them at home.

When I called them after dinner, Pete had me turn on the computer.

"Okay," he said. "Now hit Start. Do you see the list of options?"

Options?

"You mean the list of things to do?"

"That's right, Sandra, a list of options."

Sarcastic. He didn't have to be so sarcastic. (Was this the same man who'd been so sweet the night he delivered the computer to my door? Who'd spent hours teaching me the fundamentals?)

"Did you read the manual?" he demanded.

Who could read the manual? It was in some kind of mysterious language that had no relationship to the English I knew.

"I couldn't make it out," I said.

"So go and get a book." He recommended some book called *Windows for Dummies.*

Well, that did it. I hung up on him. Debby called me back.

"He doesn't have to call me a dummy," I said.

"That's the name of the book, Mom. Look, we'll be over on Sunday. Mom, you're not going to learn this overnight. Just hit Start, like Pete said."

"I don't see a start button."

"It's at the very bottom of the screen, on the left side."

"Well, it's not there now."

"It must be. How did you get into the window if you didn't hit Start?"

"I hit it, but it's not here now." I was shaking. It had disappeared and I didn't know where it went.

"Look, Mom, I can't talk anymore. Just hit Control, Alt, and Delete. That should get you out of it."

I did what she said and nothing happened. She wasn't too happy about that. "I never heard of the Start icon disappearing. You must have done something with the mouse."

Again with the mouse.

"Does that mean I can't start the computer again?"

"Well, if you lost Start, I don't see how you can work it. You'll have to wait until Sunday. Why don't you call your son, for a change?" That was a pet gripe of hers—that he got off easy while she, Pete, and Ellen were always there because they're here. And she hung up.

My son, Michael, works for the government in Washington. In some kind of think tank I can never remember the name of. I didn't like to call him at work. He's always so busy thinking. But I decided to call him and we spent an hour on the phone. (So now you know where your tax dollars are going.) We kept moving the stupid mouse around to find the Start button and the whole task bar, but it was gone. We tried this (he's such a whiz) and we tried that, and even though I couldn't get back the Start button he was very sweet about it. What can I tell you? A son is not a son-in-law. He was patience personified.

But he, too, couldn't figure out what happened to the Start button. So he told me to just hit the power button and turn it off.

"It won't break the computer?"

"It takes a lot to break a computer, Mom," he said. "Just turn it off."

I turned it off. He also recommended that I get a book, and the name didn't include the word "Dummy," so I was grateful for that.

"Well, maybe Pete can figure it out on Sunday," he said. "If not, maybe Ellen can help. It's hard to go further unless I'm at your computer."

"I'm sorry to call you at work, but I was afraid I'd break something."

"Everybody goes a little nuts at the beginning," he said.

I hung up and sat there looking at this computer. I wasn't going to let it defeat me. I was going to learn how to work it, even if I had to read a book.

Well, if that's what it took, I would have to do it, because it was obvious that Pete wasn't going to be much of a help. He felt he had given me the computer and it was my job to learn it. (God forbid, he should give me a little time.)

"I don't blame him," I told Debby diplomatically, when she called me that night. "He wasn't meant to be a teacher."

"Well, he's not strong on patience," Debby said apologetically.

"That's for sure," I said.

"What does that mean?" she asked.

"It means I'm agreeing with you," I said.

She didn't like that at all, for some reason, and before I knew it she was giving me an argument about how I never understood him or appreciated him and she was sick and tired of it. And why didn't I ever call Ellen when I had a problem? Why only her?

And she hung up on me.

Well, I was so upset that I called my daughter Ellen. And for once she answered the phone. She usually lets the answering machine pick up during the day. (She works out of her house and prefers I call her after dinner.) And I usually don't bother her during the day, because she doesn't like to be disturbed. (I'll bet if her friends called her it would be another story.) But I was so upset, I called her anyway.

Her opinion was: Number One—I shouldn't have called Pete at work; Number Two—I shouldn't have called Michael at work; Number Three—I hurt Debby's feelings; Number Four—she was working, too; Number Five—I shouldn't penalize Pete for giving me a computer; and Number Six—I should buy a book, take a class, and understand that I couldn't learn the computer overnight. And I shouldn't accuse Pete of having no patience when *I* was the one who had no patience.

This is what I called for? I hung up on her. She called me right back, but I let my answering machine take the message.

I had no intention of talking to her ever again. You bring children into this world and the minute you ask them to help, they're too busy.

Well, who needed them! I'd have to take a class. I'd have to buy a book (even though it would cost me money). I'd have to find someone who didn't jump down my throat just because I needed to learn the computer. I didn't need them. I was going to learn what Blah, Blah, Blah, Dot Com meant, if it was the last thing I did.

My mother used to say that one mother can take care of ten children, but that ten children can't take care of one mother. She was always trying to make me feel guilty for not being there with her twenty-four hours a day.

But that's another story.

The Law Makes Evening Fall

SHERRY KRAMER

(Carole is the director of a center that works with children who have learning disabilities. She is beginning to lose faith in her ability to reach and help these children, and in the society that she is helping them enter. She is smoking.)

CAROLE: The word . . . phoneme . . . is made up of five. Phonemes. Now, phonemes are the units of sound that we use to make words. You can think of them as consonants and vowels, singularly as well as in clusters, and you'd be approximately right. When we speak, we produce, on average, approximately four hundred and fifty phonemes per minute. Now if your hearing is reasonably good, you'll hear virtually all these phonemes. All four hundred and fifty of them. But no matter how good your hearing is, you will only process one hundred and fifty.

This is because hearing and processing are two different things, because hearing and understanding are two different things. As anyone who has ever tried to make anyone understand them understands. Understanding human speech is just slightly more complex a series of events than, say, putting a man on the moon. And it has to happen as fast as scooping up a handful of sand and counting each grain as it spills back onto the ground.

Fortunately, our big brain has a trick up its sleeve. It has a way to cheat, to pretend to count all the grains we miss. Too slow to actually process the rapid stream of phonemes and understand each word, our brain grabs the few words it can, and just makes the rest of them up. Yes. It just makes up twice as much meaning as it actually processes, it cheats by using clues of context, redundancy, predictability, and pattern, it—estimates meaning—the way, before radar, sailors estimated the size of an iceberg from its tip.

The sad fact is, our brains were not built to process language. This language thing is not what they were meant to do. I speak, you listen. I say a hundred words, your auditory processing system grabs a hold of thirty-three-and-a-third, and whatever meaning I might have stored in the other sixty-six or so is lost—for a split second—and then created new. By you. You are creating two-thirds of everything you hear. You are filling in all the blanks, and they are everywhere.

I speak. You listen. And we pretend that the speaker is in charge. We pretend we know who sense and meaning have to blame.

But now you know the sand. Now you know the iceberg. Now you know one-third two-thirds. Now you know my problem.

I have to rely on you for two-thirds of my story and I don't want to rely on you or anybody. I don't want to need another person for anything ever again, not for love or money and certainly, eternally, not for the truth.

But the word truth is made up of three phonemes.

So, two-thirds of the truth of my story resides in you.

Indecent Exposure

SAHRA KUPER

(Crystal is sitting in a room in the police department talking to her lawyer.)

CRYSTAL: You have to understand something. First and foremost: I needed the money. You can be my lawyer, but you—you have to know it wasn't about prestige. *(Beat. She shifts her "private part" very delicately.)* Excuse me. Curiosity maybe, sure I was curious, but not jealous or envious or anything like that. It was the money. Write that down. That is what I am saying. They offered $3,000 for this. *(She points to her groin.)* *This*— You have no idea the kind of experiments that go on in this country. I mean, you know about the lab rats, or for instance, um, the—what are those weird studies that go on at big universities? You know about those? I had done a few. I never liked working for too long at a *job* job. So, you know, I'd fill in. Do a psych experiment for a day. Get fifty bucks. Get a free meal. Are you following this? Or I'd lift weights, take some pain relievers that didn't work, and have a dead arm bent at a right angle for a week. But, you know, I'd get some more cash. It wasn't a way of life or anything. It wasn't my focus. Just something I did. Here and there.

But this one was different. For $3,000 it was highly confidential and potentially dangerous. Of course for that kind of money, you have to expect some risks. I have always been a sort of a risk-taker, run-a-muck type of a person. I know I might not look it, but it's, you know, *(she shifts again down there)* in my nature. And I was, you have to understand, well, make sure you are getting all this because I am trying to give you as much context as possible. What you have to understand is that I was working at this terrible place. Like real low class. It was a strip joint. I wasn't stripping. I mean, I don't do that, but I was a cocktail waitress and I was making terrible tips. My boss told me if I'd smile a little more . . . or, I'd . . . if I'd—well, I'm sure you are familiar with how women make tips. You can see how $3,000 would really help me get out of a rut. This rut I was in. It was time. That's how I felt. Really, well, empowered, I guess, at the thought of it. I never thought about afterwards, you know, how I would *feel*. I just wanted a fresh start. Some money in the bank, buy a nice suit, get a haircut, take a computer course. Really prepare myself for that next big step. You have to know this. It was always about the money. *(Beat)*

Well, after the operation, they had me lying in this hospital bed for weeks. Maybe months, you know I'm not sure. I was all drugged up. They wanted to test things: my flexibility, for one. Isn't that weird? A girl gets a penis and they want to know if she's more flexible? Walking was a big thing too. The way I walked. It was the only time they let me off the drugs, and thank god, or I would never have been able to escape. And the thing is, I knew what they wanted to see. They wanted to see a strut. I could just feel it. That that's what they were hungry for, that's what it was all about. So I'd do it to spite them. *(She stands up and demonstrates her walk.)* I would walk the way I walked when I was crowned Ms. Arizona. One foot delicate in front of the other.

You need to understand me emotionally, because you will have to make the court believe it wasn't just about exposing myself. *(Beat)* Once I was an upstanding citizen, you know once I had finally managed to *feel* myself again, it was like I had done it all for nothing. Here I had this big secret; this big thing between my legs and no one knew it. It *had* been about the money, it really had. But afterwards, you know, if I had to say it was about something, I guess it would be—well—I could pee standing up. Now this is just between you and me. As far as they know, I just had to go and I was going to go in my pants and it will never happen again. We have to make that clear, you and me. You and I, we will stick together on that. But I know a part of me just wanted someone to see it. And that's how I felt.

Have you ever felt that way? Like someone gives you something that would only be of value, only be real, if other people knew about it. And then that is the one thing you are never allowed to do. What a trick, you know? I mean a lady standing up to pee. How brilliant! And yet, they wanted me to hide it? I hope you see. I hope it's clear now. Because what they did, what they were expecting, what they demanded of me, it was all very cruel.

Pearls on the Moon

SHIRLEY LAURO

(Rose, middle-aged, is in her bed, permanently confined in a sanitarium in a small Midwestern town. She's speaking to her grown daughter, Ruth, who, after years of absence, has come back to visit from New York where she's a successful young poet.)

ROSE *(As to a child)*: Oh, Ruthie, baby, isn't it cool here in the yard with Mommy? Hear those cicadas, sweetheart? *(She listens.)* It means fall is coming, darling. *(She looks up.)* Such a crystal night—the stars—the big full moon—see it? *(She points and stares up at one spot.)* You know there are silly people in this world that say the moon is made of *green cheese*, baby? *(She giggles.)* And if you only *wish* on it your dreams come true? *(She laughs again, looks at Ruth.)* But they're silly-Willies, aren't they? It's made of pearls! Shiny, glistening, dewy pearls, Ruthie . . . only don't *ever* just wish on them. Only fools wish. You have to go *get* the pearls, Ruthie—if you want them. You have to climb and climb and climb—and you can do it, darling— you can do anything in this world if you have the courage. And you have it, Ruthie. I can see it in you—why you'll pull those pearls right off that silly moon when you grow up. And no one will stop you—LIKE THEY STOPPED ME—

(She turns from Ruth and slips into another time farther back in her past.) In New York—*(She looks at her fingers, suddenly nearly in tears.)* Oh how I loved New York, Ruthie, baby. They did such things—ate herring for breakfast with sour cream—rode a train under the ground! And Thomas? Oh, how I loved him! Stayed out all night—and danced and sang with him across the Brooklyn Bridge!

(To Ruth, as if she were a child again) Oh Ruthie, baby, that operation in New York wrecked everything there! See, I was only sixteen years old and he was such a handsome boy—Thomas, I mean. But the New York doctor took it out—and they sent me home and I never heard from him again and everybody knew! And nobody ever thought I'd get married or have a baby after that. But I fooled 'em. I got married and had you. And nobody laughed at me then. Why, when I was pregnant, I went down to the library every day and checked out all the books from every country in the world and read them cover to cover. "I want her to travel," I thought, "And sail the seven seas! And go round and round the world!"—then you came and your Daddy died—and everything started to change—*(She whimpers, lies back in bed, thinks for a moment, then turns back to Ruth.)* But don't *you* ever be scared of having a baby, sweetheart, hear me? Because having a baby's natural like the river—flowing with the moontides out to sea—and my child? My Ruthie? She's a moonchild with pearls in her hair—

Evelyn's Sister

DINAH LEAVITT

(Fran, just back home from her sister Evelyn's bridge club, roars on stage, carrying a box of punch cups. She removes her underwire bra from beneath her clothes.)

FRAN: I think it is a conspiracy to keep women down through physical pain. Keeping you down while they keep you up. Underwire brassieres. Today nine out of ten styles are underwires, but only a few years ago the reverse was true. Back then, underwire bras were push-up contraptions worn for low necklines. Décolletage. Not any more.

But "support," you say, for big-bosomed women. Then why are the racks full of size 28-AA underwire training bras? I'll tell you why: to train them young to suffer for some absurd, unattainable ideal of female beauty. *(She puts two punch cups over her breasts.)* Don't get me wrong, pushed-up-under-your-chin-tits are fine if you like that sort of thing, but the way you get them is painful, and we don't *all* want to suffer.

If you don't wear a bra, for whatever reason, you may not be aware of how they work—how they feel. *(She demonstrates.)* Below the cups are strips of reinforcing metal wire. Now these wires do add support, but they also press hard here. *(Points)* These are ribs. I heard about a woman who was being autopsied, and the doctor couldn't figure out the marks under her breasts. Had she been beaten? Tortured? Turned out they were underwire bra marks. It's a conspiracy, like high heels, girdles, and makeup. My sister, Evelyn, says, "Frannie, you are crazy. If you don't like underwire bras or high heels, don't wear them. Do you really even need a bra?" She doesn't get the point—these things are no longer options for the overly groomed, they are defining us. Comfortable alternatives are becoming scarcer and scarcer.

God, is it hot in here? I am so hot. At least it's not noisy. *(She puts a smock on over her clothes.)* Don't get me started on noise. Noise is other people. Boom boxes, car radios turned up so loud I hear them when I am inside with the door closed. Boom whacca whacca whacca whacca. They're all going to be deaf. They'll be cool then! I have an idea who is behind the underwire bra conspiracy, but I cannot figure out who is behind the drive-you-crazy-with-noise plot. At the department store, bong, bong, bong—some kind of employee signal the clerk told me. "We, like uh, just tune it out," she said. TVs, radios, stereos—it is as though people are frightened of silence. My sister, Evelyn? Turns on the TV when she comes in just to have the company. Nuts! And the music they play on radios now. It is so unspeakably bad—no tune, tortuous repetition, unintelligible lyrics mouthed by arrogant teenagers or aging hippies.

It is a sign of the times. Vulgar, vulgar, vulgar! Advertisements that you can't tell what is being sold by these half-naked models. There is no taste or restraint, and I understand the loss of the latter, but good taste used to be a pleasure. Of course, with the garbage on the television and the movies, it is no wonder. Sex, sex, and more sex. How can we do something perverted but fresh? Originally sick? I am sorry but I do not want frontal nudity on a fifty-foot screen. Evelyn says I need to stay away from the movies if I am offended by them.

Evelyn fails to see the bigger picture of what all of this is doing to our way of life on the planet. We have become a noisy, tacky, vulgar society. Maybe that is why underwire bras have become so popular. There is no moral fiber, no backbone. We are unconsciously substituting "wire" support. If your breasts are pushed high enough, everything must be okay. I cannot even imagine what fresh hell they have designed for us next. Whalebone corsets or some new, high-tech horror? It is a conspiracy even if I can't prove it. Here, wear one of these for ten hours and see if you don't agree. *(She holds out a bra.)*

Good Vibrations

DINAH LEAVITT

(Carla, 49-ish and a former hippy, enters carrying a basket of vibrators.)

CARLA: After my second divorce during an embarrassingly long depression, I had lunch with Alex, an old friend who in midlife quit her job as a stock broker's analyst and took up massage and astrology. She netted $100,000 last year. After I delivered the litany of how I was dealing with my depression: first drugs, then therapy, then more, but different and better, drugs, she said, "Carla, get a job, get a vibrator, get a life." I took this to mean that the job and the vibrator would produce "a life," and since I already had a job that I did not hate, I bought my first vibrator. Trudy. *(Holds it up and turns it on for a few seconds.)* Say hello to the folks, Trudy. *(Trudy hums and is then turned off.)*

I had no idea how to purchase sex aids and was even embarrassed to ask Alex. The pharmacy varieties did not look orgasmic, and I could see myself buying dozens of buzzing plastic appliances only to find them ineffectual or dangerous just as I had found the drugs that caring health professionals had prescribed ineffectual or dangerous or both. Come to think of it, my experience with men was a lot like that too. Actually, I couldn't see myself buying one at all—that is, getting through a cash transaction. The price wouldn't scan properly and the clerk would pick up the intercom and announce all over the store, "Price check please on a Triple Ripple Night Rider Deluxe-O-Vibe."

Why masturbation? With practice, the sex itself is just as good as any other way and you don't have to clean up anything, please anyone, fake anything. It feels whole, complete. Why would you not love you? Okay, it's not the real thing; but when was the last time you baked bread from scratch? Of course it would be better if some loving, sexy partner with your best interests at heart were around. He wouldn't do any of the things that drive you crazy—drink too much, watch fifty hours weekly of sports on TV, snore, pee on the floor beside the toilet, reject you. Yes, I would rather have him; I don't. Or I do, but that guy only stays around a month or so and then he turns into some other guy who slowly starts doing all the things that drive me nuts. Relationships are difficult today and let's face it, at my age, I am free-falling off the statistical charts as a desirable female. So I have a Pocket Rocket, and I am thinking of ordering an Auto Arouser that plugs into a car's cigarette lighter. The ad says they make roadside rest stops truly rejuvenating.

My last lover, Jeff, who at first was impressed with my arsenal, told me that "ultimately masturbation is an empty form of auto-eroticism—it is not love." I thought about all the faked orgasms of my twenties, the empty sex without the fake of my thirties, and I rejoiced at the loveless vibrations of my forties. Free at last, O Lord, free at last. I also thought of all the lovers who eventually got around to telling me that I wasn't having the right kind of orgasm—mine were immature. Excuse me, Dr. Freud. How come these Neanderthals hadn't heard of "The Myth of the Vaginal Orgasm"? It just makes sense—if you want to boil grits, you put the pot on the flame, not four inches away.

But . . . *(Pause)* But sometimes I am caught by something—a corny John Denver lyric or Shakespeare:

Love's not Time's fool, though rosy lips and cheeks
Within his bending sickle's compass come;
Love alters not with his brief hours and weeks,
But bears it out even to the edge of doom.

and I know I'd junk all the electro-sex shock treatments in my well-stocked closet for sex with intimacy. For love. Did we ever have that? We women? Somebody must have. *(She puts the vibrators back in the basket.)* Take it from Carla—get a job, get a vibrator, and get a life.

The Milestone
(from *Baby Dreams*)

ARDEN TERESA LEWIS

(Tracy, a single career woman, meditates upon turning thirty.)

TRACY: My father wants me to marry David Letterman. I'm a firm believer that dreams carry messages to us, and last night my father set us up on a blind date. David and I . . . I had the best time. Then I woke up. You know, when I was thirteen I remember sitting on my father's lap and explaining to him how the sixties revolution had entirely screwed up any chance for my happiness, because all I wanted was to marry someone wonderful and make a home for him and all our children. But my mom made me feel guilty, so I gave that up to pursue a career. But maybe I'm still hung up on being Daddy's little girl? That's stupid. But take my sister, Myra. It's as if she and I grew up in completely different families. She has the blessed birth date of 1965, a husband who loves her, an adorable little girl, house, part-time job, cars, cats. I resent everything she stands for. She's copping out. No, wait, I love Myra. I think she's the luckiest girl in the world. My mother thinks Myra is lazy. She should get a real job. My mother thinks I'm too driven. I should get a real boyfriend. My dad's worried. See, in a couple of minutes I'm going to turn thirty, and I haven't gone after any of the things I told him I wanted when I was thirteen. Because I don't want them now. I am thirty years old, so now I have baby dreams. Having a baby would definitely ruin my chances with David Letterman. Thirty. A small milestone, but a pivotal hormonal transition nonetheless. Yesterday I was a vibrant, free spirit. Today I'm a desperate woman looking for commitment. I was an independent, working professional. Now I'm a sexless, workaholic candidate for osteoporosis. Once a nubile, sensuous woman. Now a walking time bomb. Except I won't explode. I'll just shrivel up slowly, along with my ovaries. The first step toward spinsterhood has been taken. Or, the beginning of a decade of possibilities. I mean, these are the nineties, and a girl's aging is not the trauma it used to be—it's worse. We used to be totally ignored. Cloistered. Shut away. Left alone. Now, we're magnified, under glass, so the cells of our skin can be injected, plumped, exfoliated, shrunk, dermabrazed, and then wrapped in tiny time-release caplets that attack you in the night so you wake refreshed, revived, and regressed to the age of infancy so you can feel again like a baby's behind! Help me! Please! Somebody impregnate me, I'm melting!

Flying

CAROL K. MACK

(During the following relived memory, Kay, 19, very bright, vulnerable, quirky, transforms from human to bird. She may be speaking to us in her Post-Avian state from a place on the lawn of her school or home or hospital. Wherever she is, she is alone and she wants us to understand her story. The birdlike mannerisms that express themselves throughout the story and that finally overwhelm her are to be invented by the actress.)

KAY: OK, here's the hard part . . . OK, a couple of months ago? When I was human, that's when it all started. Right in front of the student center on February 10th at three o'clock. The bells on the campus chapel were going off, which is how I know the time. Anyhow, I was just standing there when I saw this feather. It was lying on the snow? *(She reaches down, picks it up, examines it.)* It was white as the snow so it was nearly invisible. And it had these . . . markings. This weird blue design on the underside, almost like a code, and it . . . well, it smelled so familiar, and that's when it hit me. This was all a message. And for the first time in my life, everything fell into place. I realized . . . I knew that my real father was a bird. *(Shifts uncomfortably, lifting her elbows, shoulders.)*

So then what? I mean I knew I'd have to confront my mom with this. But she'd never admit it. She hates talking about what she calls "closed chapters" of her life? That includes a lotta stuff. I mean was it a one-night stand? And how could she forget? My mom is so . . . How could I ask her about transpecies lovers? And there are other questions. DNA-related ones. Like, could I fly? I mean at *that* point I still didn't know. *(Moves around, slightly more avian, annoyed at the memory.)*

The day before the feather, I had, coincidentally, picked my freshman term-paper topic from this list of choices and of *course* I picked Quetzalcoatl! I always had this, connection, to Quetzalcoatl, y'know, that gorgeous Aztec plumed serpent god. But this bitch, Ashley Williams? She claimed her great-great-grandmother was one-eighth Guatemalan, and she picked Quetzalcoatl too. So the professor told me that since the Aztecs were really more Ashley's than mine, why didn't I think about Druids or something!? I said to Tim, "It's not fair!" "Life's not fair, mate," Tim said. He used to call my roommate "mate," too, when they were dating. So I never know—is it 'cause he gets us mixed up or 'cause he's from Australia? Everybody's from somewhere but me . . . *(She crosses her arms, flaps her elbows.)* Bummer.

Before the feather it was such a totally shitty year. My roommate freaked out and dropped out and then I moved in with her ex, Tim. He has this gorgeously unpronounceable name and is so . . . intense, and he's also very cute. All I wanted was a name like his, with two clinking consonants at the top that linked me to some exotic ancient land. Something mysterious to sign my papers with. A name with maybe only clicks. A name that if you said it the wrong way would mean something like fart. But being from Long Island, well, like Tim says, that's Kansas. It's all Kansas, mate. *(Growing indignant and "ruffled.")*

So, anyhow, it was this very next day that my dad sent me his message by feather, and it wasn't long before "Kay Smith," in what looks like an ordinary human body, is utterly transformed. I began to hover, mentally at first, and in the library. I began hunting for my roots, my *own* folk culture, back to the first soaring Archaeopteryx! *(Fascinated, enthusiastic)* My dad's ancestral superiority is pretty evident! He had visual acuity way beyond human. And what about those impossible migratory navigational feats with no maps at all! Probably the most important find is this organ called the amygdala. It's this perfect snug core coiled way deep inside every single human brain. What does it do? It gives you this adrenal rush the minute an identifiable Other comes into view. *(Triumphantly)* And it's *mine*. It's MINE. I've got the original! It's *pre-mammal*! It's this amygdala that's like the most important thing on campus! This amazing organ is more part of my heritage than my classmates' and never given credit! Ignored! But this very amygdala practically rules the roost and not just for *sex*, but even for *(looking around)* who you sit with in the cafeteria! Me? *(Perches, rolling her shoulders)* I sit by myself!

And I begin to think a lot about flying. *(Romantically)* Now that I'm no longer "Kay," who am I? I mean my real name must be so ancient a sound it couldn't even be represented by glyph! It's indecipherable, just a wingbrush, maybe a feathery noise like a breeze or a whisper. I wore my beautiful white feather at all times under my T-shirt, folded in my bra, near my heart. Hidden. *(Annoyed)* Of course I avoided wearing it in any fashion that I realized was just plain plumage display. Somebody might think it was some kind of Native American rip-off. It's not! And it's not Kabbalah, either! It's a Bird Thing! OK? Anyhow, as an Avian creature I am Beyond Culture. And also am totally beyond guilt for ever being anywhere where anybody was oppressed anytime in history 'cause my dad's folks' folks? were originally connected to the Great Auk. And the Great Auk lived on all these uninhabited isles and developed a near mythic reputation. But, well, that's only a guess. Dad may have been a swan.

To attempt to be true to my heritage I started to eat only trail mix. Tim said, "Losing weight, mate?" And I thought, what a jerk! What a jerk. Bird weight gain and loss is all *timing*. It's all about Nesting and Migration—why bother, he'd never understand. I just blinked at him. Then I realized I hadn't blinked in a week! You know what that means. Also I noticed this feeling of tension in my shoulder blades. I didn't know if it was stress and my knapsack or some latent sprouting at the base of my blades.

And I was just blown away by thinking about my amazing dad—I mean when I think about his air sacs, his fused hips, his great scaly feet, a *faster* heartbeat, air in his bones, and at least *three* times as many vertebrae in his neck! All these Avian traits filled me with such pride I could hardly keep from crowing. And to think that humans denigrate these glorious creatures with names like "secretary bird" and "grebes"!? And how about "crazy as a loon"? Or that really odious comparison of vultures to lawyers! *(Angry determination)* I'll redress this. Yes. Why, we're everybody's icon: the eagle, the falcon, the dove! There's no ceiling on bird power. And where does Nietzsche come off using the eagle as if he had some inside track? You wish, Nietzsche! And Edgar Allen Poe. Nevermore!

My paper's due, and I decide to present my own topic— it's gonna be all about bird sound and finally show how to talk to a bird. I know now. I can caw and warble. In bed I make new burry noises in my throat that scare Tim!

It was during finals, I "fixed on" the crowd sitting in their little tribal formations in the cafeteria. I decided right then to eliminate my memories and thus gain the necessary lightness for a demonstration. *(Getting up on a bench, excitedly)* I concentrated on my hidden feather, visualizing it a thousand fold, and when all I could see were white feathers with faint blue markings, I imagined myself covered with them, and I climbed onto my corner table and I rose up into the air! *(Arms spread, awe)*

It was in this final soaring flight to the cafeteria ceiling, a burst of energy and weightlessness, that I first became aware of this sound under me. *(Still, awe)* The sounds rise unlike anything else in the universe! Each voice utterly unique, each vibration like no other in all time. And yes, YES, greater than any birdsong! It is this chorus of human voices that forms the up-current on which I glide. By human hum I hover, and I look down at all those eyes looking back at me! Those eyes. They're all filled with expression and each pair unlike any other pair, without the Avian brilliance or opaqueness—why they're filled with wonder at my flight! *(Blinks away the humanity.)* OH! I try a new bird squint, first raising my powerful lower eyelid halfway up, then sliding the nictitating membrane, my third eyelid, horizontally across. I discover the use of this membrane which has eluded human ornithologists: what it does is filter the field of vision. OH! Now I can see all those amazing eyes with birdsight! They're like a shimmering lake, a continuum of light facets! OH! How incredible!

(In a very different tone) That was my last conscious thought before I fell down near the hot trays. . . . *(Moves to another place)*

When I wake up, Tim's kneeling next to the doctor, looking worried. I try to speak, my *beak* . . . can't get my beak around the words. Nobody can hear me. Tim shrugs and he's swinging his ponytail, saying, "I dunno, mate. Magical realism?"

And then I look around and they're all looking so, help-less, so . . . sad and worried, all my old classmates, so amaz-ingly different, each of them. My Avian Pride dies right then. A tear drops onto my T-shirt. Human! Birds can't cry. But then I see the tear roll down my arm, and I see the downy underfeathers sprouting now as my arm turns wing. Too late. Too late. I'm speechless, and I feel only love. Love. Oh, I wish I could communicate with the species!

Excerpt from *Animal Dreams*

JENNIFER MAISEL

(Natalie is dressed in a hospital gown. Behind her, a hospital bed holds an image of her body in fetal position. Natalie looks down at her body. There is the sound of whirring machinery.)

NATALIE: I don't recognize that body at all. I mean even if you were to take me into a lineup of bodies and force me choose . . . It's so . . . slack, soft tired skin. Look at that razor stubble—I mean the legs. I used to let the legs go an extra day or two but I always shaved under the arms. I didn't like the way it looked when I didn't shave under the arms. I smelled a little rancid too when I didn't. That is one sorry-looking case. *(Looks around her to call)* Could someone around here just take a minute and, y'know, shave her under the arms please? It would only take a minute. Look, you get so convinced she can hear you, that she could respond if only given the right stimulus, give her a little dignity, why don't you?

Oh, to hell with it.

All the positions you put your body in over a lifetime and when push comes to shove this is the one it chooses to remember. It's a good cliché, but not all that comfortable without the waves in the amniotic fluid keeping you afloat. *(To the body on the bed)* Why don't you revert back to one of the good positions, huh? Don't you remember any of the good ones? Try this one. *(She perches on the stool, legs up and splayed apart, head back.)* Oh c'mon, this one always worked. What about—*(Gets off the stool and bends over it, looking back coyly over her shoulder. Tries a look of passion.)* You are no fun at all. You've gotta remember. It hasn't been that long, has it? The body's supposed to remember these things. Like a bicycle, right?

They're not sure whose hand they hold. They're not sure whether it can hear them. They're not sure if they're doing any good at all. They're not sure if they know who she is anymore. They can label her—parts of what she was—Mom. Lover. Wife. Bitch. Sixth-Grade Teacher. Friend . . . Patient . . . Statistic.

They're not sure if she *is* anymore.

(A school bell rings. As a teacher.) According to the medical profession a coma is the state from which a person cannot be aroused. According to the medical profession there are fifteen stages of coma—stage 1 showing no response to the outside world and stage 15 the most . . . social. According to the medical profession, Glascow's fifteen-point coma scale is also a crock of shit. It just depends on who you talk to.

Maybe we're just too tired to wake up. Maybe it's just not worth the effort. Maybe there's a comfort in the deep irreverence of ignoring the commotion and the congestion of the everyday. Maybe it's just too painful to be awake right now. Maybe it's time to heal. Maybe I just need a fucking rest! I need a fucking rest!

(Composes herself.) In the deep stages I've been able to escape the body and watch the remnants of it metastasizing into one connected mass of small cancerous lumps. I keep my eyes focused inward and note the proliferation of cells like a dandelion patch gone wild and I blow one small tumor into pieces that take root where they fall. I make a wish. And I walk through the inside of my body noting the holocaust of my being, the radiation having killed the healthy and not the sick, the florid growth, the blood full of lumpy cells. And I notice, my wish hasn't come true. This is still the body they say belongs to me.

Celia, my daughter, sits by me and tells me it's OK to let go. To let go. It's OK to let go. How the fuck do you know. Trying to get rid of me? . . . How do you know it's OK? What if I let go and there's nothing? What if I let go to nothing? Hold tight! *(Extends hands in front of her. Four irregular breaths. Four more regular breaths.)*

Your hand is warm. I can feel that tic of blood at the bottom of your thumb. I'd put my lips there when you were a baby. You wonder if I like it here. You wonder if I know you. You wonder if I know where I am. Don't let go! Don't bring me out of it. It will hurt. God! If you bring me out of it, it will hurt. I'm not coming out of it again. Do you hear me? I am not coming out of it again. Don't let go of my hands now. You brought me back in here. Don't let go of them. . . .

You know as much as they tell you about the inevitability of fate—you are very concerned because you don't want to end up like me. You tell people you take care of yourself. You say it's not heredity but environment. You say—

Don't let go of my hands. Do not let go of my hands, young lady. You little bitch. You little bitch. Where do you think you're going? Come back here. Come back here.

Things I can tell you that you just might not know:

There are times when I am trapped in my body in a heavy stupor. One of those stupors like after a really bad drunk. One of those times you struggle to get to the surface only to find out it's not the place that you want to be.

There are times when I'm not in my life as it is anymore but as it was. I am teaching. I am falling in love again. I'm watching Mom die.

My body lets me go. I am in the room, I am on the street, I am flying over the world seeing places I never made it to. I am visiting the people I love and they feel me there but they can't quite put a name to it.

My body lets me go. I want to kick it. I want to punch it. I want to scratch great holes in the skin and watch the blood well up. I want to pinch it black and blue and scream, "You goddamn miserable thing, what good have you been for me? What the fuck have you been doing to me? How dare you betray me like this? How dare you?"

But I can't bite and I can't tear or scratch. My body lets me go and the freedom becomes unbearable and I want to be back inside the confines of my body, if only to know my limitations.

I guess you just have to be there.

(To her husband) Oh . . . What are you doing here? You hate hospitals. You hate antiseptic smell not really masking, cotton swabs, TVs positioned high above the bed. You hate me. You live that moment when your hand grasped the . . . breast . . . over and over. It was sex, it was skin, it was touching, absorbing, culminating . . . like so many times before, so many times before, we don't have to speak . . . we've never had to speak. Then you say . . . "What's that? Feel that. What's that? Feel that." Ruined the mood, I can say that much. This is how you'll remember me now.

(School bells rings. As teacher speaking in a student's voice.) I was going to bring something very special to show and tell today, teacher, but I must have lost them on the way. No I did, really, look. *(She bares her chest, showing two big scars winding where her breasts used to be.)* I'll look for them and bring them tomorrow, I promise. They must be around here somewhere. I'll look real hard. I swear. *(School bell rings again.)*

I wonder. I wonder when they tell me about the cancer—is this the wrong thing to be happening to my body? Maybe it's the right thing, maybe it's the only reaction to the world my body can have, maybe it's the only way it can express itself, make itself heard, going out of control, multiplying chaos, anarchy. We try to contain the revolution of cells with knives and poisons and affirmations. What if those cells are my battle against the world? A way of growing stronger to combat the daily and the lifelong, to make more of just me against the world. What if I somehow agreed to let the doctor cut out my strength?

(The machine whirring grows louder.)

They say go into the light. They say come back to us. I can't. I can't.

If I just stay here. If I just stay here. If I could just stay here.

(The sounds of the machinery . . . the heart monitor, the dripping, take over as the world around Natalie becomes dark. . . .)

The Last Bridge

MELISSA MARTIN

(Marge, fifteen, crouches on the floor of her bedroom, staring at a teen magazine. Suddenly threatened and repulsed, her body convulses slightly. She opens her mouth in a huge, silent scream and then gags. Nothing comes out. She sticks her tongue out as far as possible, and then gags again, still staring at the magazine, but nothing happens. She pants and heaves, and then, explodes.)

MARGE: AAAAAHH . . . Oh, gross out! Have to look . . . away. OH GOD . . . I can't . . . but I . . . GOTTA!!! AAAHHHH! AAAAHHH! LOOK! IT'S REALLY THERE!!! It's on your pants, Donny. A little sliver of a moon, a shadow there on . . . On your snow white . . . white—white, kianna—CROTCH!!! *(She wraps her arms about her body, rocks back and forth on her knees nearly keening.)* You've been hanging there in that same perfect two-dimensional lunge since the March issue of *Tiger Beat* came out eleven whole days ago. And I've been here on my bed admiring the thirty-six yous, every one adoring me, but why didn't I notice the SHADOW? The little blip, that darker zone around the lighter zone that is there because . . . You have a lump . . . a lump—a lump—a bulge. YOU HAVE SOMETHING IN YOUR PANTS DONNY OSMOND! *(Pause)* I have to tell Rosetta I accidentally discovered that Donny Osmond, my Ken Doll—my poster boy has a . . . a . . . what am I going to call it so she doesn't drop and blow lunch—God knows *I'm* going to every time I see the dirty sticky spots where there used to be tape holding up my thirty-six yous. Because, you gotta come down, Donny, now—all of you! Oh, Oow—oow—o pain, pain . . . I have to find a word for this, Rosetta. I only know words like . . . "ding-a-ling," and . . . "wiener." With "ding-a-ling" there's the horrifying wiggling that you can't help but think about, which is nothing compared to the—the sound effects! AAAHHH! AAHH! AAAHHH! And needless to say, except like now, with "wiener" there's the, uh, the unavoidable eating thing. Oh, RALPH. I swear to God, Donny, this is all my grandmother's fault—at lunch time she'd ask, "Are you SURE you wouldn't like a wee-nie?" Could she say "hot dog"? No! And what did she want to name my puppy? "BONER"! Right there at Sunday dinner, "Honey, why don't you name the little guy BONER?" HOW THE FUCK AM I EVER SUPPOSED TO BE NORMAL? Is it any wonder that I'm gonna end a six-year love affair with a poster because I finally realized he had a penis?!!

(Pause. Then a horrified intake of air. A big discovery.) Hear that? I said "penis." Peeenniiisss. It's so sinister sounding, the p's and s's. Peeeeeennnnniiiiissss. Saying it is almost as bad as see-ing it, not the shadowed, covered bump—the real thing! Which is to say nothing of . . . touching one. *(Whispered)* Oh oh oh oh! Please God, I know they all have them, even Donny, please God save me from ever having to touch a penis . . .

I Know Me

MARY BETH MASLOWSKI

(Carla is downstage in a spotlight. She is uneasy but trying hard to be strong. There is a chair behind her. The rest of the set is in darkness.)

CARLA: Oh, yes, thank you. *(She pulls the chair over and sits and looks nervously around.)* No, I've never been on public assistance before. It's the first time for me and my family and it wasn't easy I can tell you that. Coming here I mean. My kids are young so they have no idea what's going on. It's probably better that way. My husband and I decided to get divorced, you see. Anyway, I don't want *anything* from him, well maybe just a little money for the kids, that's only fair, but it still wouldn't be enough. . . . Excuse me? Yes, I do live over in Parson's Creek but . . . well, the thing is, I've thought about it and we're going to move here to Albertsville, I mean if we can. . . . No, we don't have family here. I don't know anyone here except Dr. . . . um, a doctor here . . . Why do I wanna move here? Well, now it gets a little embarrassing. I thought about this real hard. I said to myself, okay, that's it. I'm leaving Jim, that's my husband. I have to move on for me and for the sake of my kids. And when I had decided that, it was like a whole world opened up. I picked up the newspaper to find us a new place to live. I couldn't stay with him. And let me tell you, it felt so good to take some action. I even went with the kids to look at a few places. You don't know what a feeling it was. Suddenly all this strength and power and really feeling like hey, I can do this and to hell, um, heck with Jim and it was just so right. I wouldn't want to take this money forever, no Ma'am. I want to work. I like to work. Before I got married I was a salesgirl at Winter's department store . . . What? *(Slowly)* Why didn't I apply at the office in Parson's Creek? . . . Well, this is really hard for me to say, and mind you, I don't think I'm a proud person but, if I can get this, um, public assistance I think, *no*, I'm sure I wouldn't be able to stay in Parson's Creek. I don't know, you might think I'm crazy, or, you may hear this all the time, it's just that I know me and I tried to walk into the office at home but I couldn't do it. I'm not stuck up or nothing, really I'm not. But I was walkin' down Elm Street, that's where the office is, but you probably know that already. So I'm there on Elm pushing Jen in the stroller and trying to look all casual and nice like nothing is going on, and I walk by the office there and I look around and I see Edna Robinson across the street. So then I panic and I realize I can't walk in there with Edna Robinson seeing me. I started to get all nervous that I'm even near the building so I speed up and go into the Dunkin' Donuts a couple of doors down and I buy a donut for me and Jen even though I wasn't hungry. But that doesn't mean I waste money or anything, 'cause I don't. I'm real careful. This shirt here I'm wearing, I've had it for . . . huh? Edna? Oh, she's one of the mothers from Billy's class, and, well, you know, it's a pretty small town and . . . *(Nodding)* Oh yes, of course you're right. I have nothing to be ashamed of. I know it's not my fault and isn't it just a blessing that there is some place that people who are having trouble can go to. And trust me I wish it was different. I wish I could walk into that office with my head held high and just go up to the counter unashamed, but I know me, you see. *(She looks down and pauses.)* I tried again though. This is how important it was to me. I sat and ate my donut real slow and walked out again. I looked, didn't see anybody I knew. I held my head up and was just gonna turn into the doors when I thought I saw my neighbor Dee Dee driving down the street. I wasn't sure but it looked like her and I was almost positive that was her faded blue Chevy and then I thought of what she said to me. What she said about going into the local supermarket and paying for my groceries with food stamps. I can't imagine it and oh, you probably think I'm some silly woman who thinks she's too good for this world and I don't even know if I could do it somewhere else but I have to try and, hmmm? . . . Really? Well I can imagine you could have heard this before. I'm gonna go back to work though, that's my plan. Soon as Jen is ready for school.

Noon Day Sun

CASSANDRA MEDLEY

(Zena is a very fair-skinned black woman living in 1957. As she dresses for a formal reception, she recalls a memory.)

ZENA: All it took was for me to step up to the platform, climb them three iron steps to the train . . . somebody's hands already helping me with my . . . "our" . . . suitcase, swinging it on the rack above my head. Seats so full for that time of early morning . . . all sorts of colored faces all headed to Memphis or, like me, points further North . . . families crowded in together, ropes holding their few belongings inside overstuffed boxes . . . smells of cold fried chicken, wrapped in oilskin, made the night before, faces friendly . . . smiling folks . . . Colored people headed for . . . Paradise up "North" . . . *(Zena holds out her hand as if offering a ticket.)* He reaching for my ticket like he did for everybody else . . . *(She extends her hand in an offering gesture.)* I always thought that when and if God was to ever come to test us, that it would be . . . I dunno . . . well, like some moment full of thunder . . . some flash of brightness striking you blind in the face, like Reverend Thomas preached about St. Paul struck down on his way to Damascus. . . . *(Pause)* But no . . . when it finally does happen? It can be so simple, so quiet. See, God can slip a test right in between your breath and you not even know till you're looking back from behind you. See he noticed me. . . . He suddenly "saw" me, or "thought" he saw me. And he tipped his hat. *(She nods.)* And not leering, not despising. No, 'cause he's thinking he's seeing a "lady." And him "seeing" me, made me suddenly "somebody" deserving to be seen. *(In conductor's voice)* "'Cuse me, M'am, but you done made a terrible

95

mistake . . ." *(In her own voice)* "Mistake?" But my ticket's paid in full! Is this the wrong train? I'm headed for Memphis and due North . . . What . . . is there some . . . *(In conductor's voice)* "Naw, naw, pretty Miss, don't get excited. But this here's the nigger coach, ain't you noticed it? You want the car up front that's reserved for our white clientele, follow me . . . right this way. . . ." *(Resuming her own voice)* And there it was. God's test so fast, so easy, so . . . surprising and simple, I barely had a moment to feel myself taking in air. Handed my "magic carpet" by some red-faced, pug-nosed fool who was "doing his duty" for the purity of his race. Ha. *(Pause)* Felt like I was moving and standing still at the same time. He lifted my suitcase for me like I was the genuine lady he believed me to be. *(Pause)* And I walked down that aisle past all the rest of us Colored . . . watching me in silence . . . past the smirks on their faces . . . past eyes . . . and if bitterness could cut they would have slashed me. *(Pause)* Well, I just keep walking forward . . . straight ahead . . . and from that day to this I never look behind, I just keep walking.

Human Affairs

SUSAN MILLER

(Slim, a woman in her thirties, nicknamed because she has the style and wit of those great movie stars of an earlier black-and-white era, sits at a cabaret table with her female lover, who has just finished singing, and their two male friends, also lovers, who have brought up the delicate subject of gay marriage.)

SLIM: Looking for someone, longing for someone. It's every-one's question. That and how am I going to die. *(Beat)* There's this one inescapable and encompassing thing you have. Which is yourself. So the question, which belongs to every-one, which is everyone's to ask, is—who is going to be with me? Who is going to make it less terrible to be me? *(Beat)*

I saw this article. About lesbian sex. About how penetra-tion was really a big part of lesbian sex. And I—I was like—what is lesbian sex? See, I don't have lesbian sex. I have personal sex. I have sex with another person. That's the sex I have. When I have it. I like to think nobody is having any kind of sex when I'm having it. When I'm making love, I mean, I don't like to think anyone else is. Or even knows what it is. I don't like to think that anyone else is doing what I'm doing. In any way. I mean the whole idea of gay marriage—why do we have to take a position? I'm frankly sick of that. I'm saying, have your life. Do whatever. Do anything. Do something. I'm so fatigued by what are now deemed issues. Don't put us in the context of something, okay. Don't—don't—I love you, all right. I thrill to hear what you have to tell me. When I see you—when I see you, I think—well, I don't think, what is your stand? Suddenly we're a topic. I'm worried how this is what we've become.

You want to hold someone. You want to make someone part of your family. You want to dedicate your novel or something to someone. Your full-to-the-brimming heart is now part of a group's public posture or a social wave or some act of congress. You see it against a backdrop of some attenuated tradition, and after all, what are you if not an iconoclast. You have to be for it or against it. Your spokespeople tell you this or that. *(Beat)* You want to belong to the world with someone else. Not you want to belong like you're some outcast. You just want—belonging. *(Pause)*

Anyway you don't have to have gay marriage or lesbian sex. You can't actually have it. It isn't haveable. There is only what you do, what you do with someone else. How you act.

Excerpt from *Bugaboo*

RACHELLE MINKOFF

(Irene, a college student, reads aloud from her paper. She is shaky at first.)

IRENE: "Two of the characters we have studied this year took their lives into their own hands. How would you like it if, after committing suicide, you found yourself just starting over in the same life, only a little further back, and unable to make a single change?" *(She takes a deep breath, grows steady.)* I think that would be comforting to me. Somehow. That it wasn't, couldn't have been, possible for me to do anything different. That I wouldn't have wanted to. That I wasn't all wrong, and just fill in the blank—repressed, uptight, rebellious, boy crazy—something—anything but what I should have been— cool, knowing, adept, on the right track, aware, oh I don't know—sexual. I'm afraid of saying sexual—that is, sexually involved at an earlier age—as though I hadn't wanted to be. But then, but that's the problem—I did want to be, and nobody wanted me. And if only someone had wanted me, I would have been different, I would have been the kind people wanted, and so people would have wanted me, and would want me. But I'm repeating myself and I promised myself I wouldn't. What I'm trying to say is I have wanted all my life only to be wanted and I don't want anyone to know just how unwantable I am. I saw a play once where one character said to another: You know what your problem is? You didn't have sex when you were in high school. And it wasn't just a charac- ter saying it—it was clearly the author speaking through his character of choice against the character he abhorred. And though I knew this had been a juvenile thought—what he had just expressed—I thought—he's right—he's right—this writer writing this play who is so admired and cool and gets to be a writer (something I want to be but can't 'cause nobody wants me)—he's right what's wrong with me is I didn't have sex when I was in high school and what's more is it's something I can't change—something I'll never be able to change—I'll always be somebody who isn't anybody because I never had sex in high school. It's like Freud saying people were successful if their mothers loved them. Well then should I just give up? I have a friend she's perfect. And she spent two years—two years in therapy—once every other week on and off for two years and was able in the end to leave because she realized her mother really did love her after all, and so, in addition to being perfect in everything else because her mother loved her, she was even good at therapy because her mother loved her. And what's more, her mother loved her. And all of it because she was loveable which I'm not.

The Baptist Gourmet

JILL MORLEY

(Tulula has her own cable cooking show. She is Southern—probably from South Carolina or New Orleans.)

TULULA: G'Mornin! Welcome to Channel 64's "Cookin' with Tulula." I'm Tulula Lee May, your Baptist Gourmet and before I lead you in a recipe, I'm gonna lead you in a prayer.

Lordy, Lordy, let me learn. Not to let my souffle burn. And if it does, oh promise me this. Someone in my kitchen will like it crisp! Amen.

Last night, I was divinely inspired when the Lord came to me in a dream and he said, "Tulula, you are my culinary link to humanity. I bestow upon you the celestial preparation for fried grits."

Ingredients are hominy, cheese, and the life-giving energy to all the Lord's creatures . . . fat.

First you must baptize your ingredients. *(Throws water on the ingredients with fervor)* You're baptized! You're baptized! You're baptized!

Next, we finely chop the hominy and the cheese, which I already have done because they won't let me have the air time I need. *(Smiles and winks at a producer offstage)* Isn't that right, Jimmy? *(Under her breath)* Producer Shmoducer.

Then, we take the hominy, the cheese, we put it in a skillet and FRY IT UP!!! JUST FRY IT UP! IN THE NAME OF THE LORD, JUST FRY IT UP!!!!

(Lightheaded, she sits down and fans herself.) Oh, this is gonna be a good one.

Now, while we're waitin' for the culinary miracle, like waitin' for the second coming, I'd like to read some of my viewer mail. Preacher Mapplethorpe writes, "Dear Tulula, thank you for bringing that fried Caesar's salad to the church bazaar last week. Everyone raved over those cute little baby Jesus croutons. And that parmesan cheese looked like snow in the manger!"

Amen.

Tessie Jo Miller from Duncan Road asks, "Dear Tulula, what is the rule of thumb in Southern Baptist food preparation?" Tessie, has your cheese dun slid off your cracker? Just slap on some cheese and FRY IT UP! FRY IT UP! IN THE NAME OF THE LORD, JUST FRY IT! *(Collapses and fans herself again)* Lord save us all.

Letter from Madge Peeker on Winston Lane, "How do I make my home fried taters taste like yours?" Madge, I seen the way you fry those taters at the church socials. You just chop 'em all up like they was the devil's spawn! With each slice, you must instill goodness and ethics and morality. Handle your taters the way God handles His children and your creation will be as perfect as His. On that note, let's resurrect those grits. . . . *(She tastes them.)* Mmmmmmm, mmmmmmm, just like the Lord woulda made them.

Now, tell your Catholic friends to tune in next week because I'm making fried St. Joan Kabobs! Bye y'all!!!

The Interview

JILL MORLEY

(Laura is an insecure actress with a dark brooding temperament. She is in for an interview with a casting director.)

LAURA: Don't you have a scene for me to read? I am so boring. I am not one of these personality actresses. I'm completely devoid of personality. You're probably looking for one of those fun-loving, festive girls and that's not me. You see, I don't wear green on St. Patrick's Day. I'm not the kind of girl who dresses for the holidays.

I'm anti-holiday.

I don't know what it is. . . . I have friends. They like me. I'm not even shy. Just . . . When I was in the third grade, I wrote an essay for my teacher, Miss Laskowski. The theme was, "I'll Never Forget The Day . . ."

I wrote something like, "I'll never forget the day my father bought us ducklings. It was such a surprise. The smallest one was Milk. The next smallest was Quackers. The biggest was Harold. Milk was the first one to die. . . ."

I went on to coldly describe how each one of them got killed by my dog. I was a dark kid.

In the margin, Miss Laskowski wrote, "I enjoyed your story! Very good."

She probably thought I would grow up to be an axe murderer. But instead, here I am, an actress. *(Laughs nervously)*

Oh! I started working this receptionist job but I'm terrible! I'm not built to "receive" people. I can't synthesize a genuine smile to random people, strangers. Who cares? I don't know them and the temp agency certainly isn't paying me the big bucks.

Are you sure you don't want me to read something? I really feel uncomfortable. . . . A scene? A poem? The telephone book? Because even that is going to be more interesting than . . . excuse me . . . can I do a monologue?

Southernmost Tip

JANET NEIPRIS

(In the garden of Ernest Hemingway's house in Key West, Florida. Georgia, a young woman, is speaking to Michelangelo Schwartz, a young sculptor.)

This was the moment when I knew nothing was working. I was having lunch at the Four Seasons with an important client. He was a member of a Swiss banking family. He was young, chic, and available. I was seated at the best table in the Pool Room—*away* from the service, *away* from the door, *away* from the spray of the fountain. I had on my newest Calvin Klein outfit in Banana Republic beige. My handbag was a Louis Vuitton, my shoes were Ferragamo. I ordered the bagatelles of lobster, the most expensive item on the menu, and I didn't care. In the room, people passed to and fro and nodded discreetly. I was among friends. I had everything. And I was miserable. *(Beat)* The night before, my new VCR had arrived. It was sleek, black, beautiful, and digitally operated. I prepared a snack of Paul Newman's own popcorn in my microwave, and settled down to a favorite that I'd had delivered by my video club . . . *Thelma and Louise*. So there I lay, on the new Ralph Lauren sheets, surrounded by seventeen small pillows. I collect pillows . . . white lace from France, hand-painted silk from the Orient . . . and Thelma and Louise are being chased by all these police cars, from every direction, and all these lights are flashing, and Thelma asks Louise, "How far are we from Mexico?" And Louise says, "About two hundred and fifty miles" . . . and Thelma asks, "How long will that take?" but we know they're never going to get there, to Mexico . . . this is on the TV—

And then they're surrounded and it's for sure they're gonna be caught and Louise is really giving it the gas, and then Thelma is saying to Louise, "Louise, no matter what happens, I'm glad I'm with you," and I begin to cry. And all because Thelma's saying this to Louise—this is before they sail the car over the cliff into the Grand Canyon—and B. B. King music is playing and Louise asks Thelma if she has her seat belt on and I'm crying more, but I don't think that was why I was crying . . . But I didn't know why.

Sleepwalkers

PENNY O CONNOR

(Clare, late thirties, appears to be quiet, cool, emotionally removed. She was left at home with her mother, while her sister Sara left for university.)

CLARE: The nature of suffocation.

There is a moment between our fishy existence and our first breath when our whole world has squeezed around us and pushed us out when we must be suffocating. The waters break and the slimy walls which we are touching come further in on us, squeezing hard insistently, ejecting us, rejecting us, decreasing the space. Nowhere to go but out, out into the light, out into the gravitational field, and the cord, this thick nourishing cable is cut, sawed, bitten, chewed through, hacked—snip! The cut of the first breath, air pressure forcing its way into our vacuum lungs and we scream, "Aaaagh, aaagh, aagh"—released from our suffocation. "You have a beautiful little girl, Mrs. Eve, a beautiful little girl." A red-faced, bald wrinkled shrimp of a thing, screaming. Look at her tiny fingernails—perfectly formed—just like you, she has your ears, your eyes, your nose, your mouth, your ugly temper, your foul-mouthed, gut-wrenching stench, and she gurgles just like you. She has everything of you and she has taken you away. You no longer exist. You stamp your pattern on her little form, knit her soul a tight little jumper and everyone laughs—"She's just like her mother, just like her mother!" The Piscean fish swallows the bait. Chameleon tendencies—Miss and Mrs. Eve. Passing the buck from generation to generation, handed on, running the same track, a relay race never ending, circular, fresh energy, new souls to keep it going. The same and not the same. Doesn't time fly? Here's my baton of genes and social conditioning, and the two run side by side till one tires and drops out. Suffocation of souls in the earthly body, imprisonment, restriction, from fish to mammal and no wings to fly. I have my chameleon tendencies. The part of Miss Eve is relatively easy. Her mother's daughter. All that I most hate paraded in front of me, day after day, no letup. Suffocation.

The grotesque mirrors in the fun fair, and how we howl with laughter, how we howl with laughter. Ha ha ho ho.

The suffocation of what passes for love. Do this, do that, or I won't love you anymore. Two breathing the same air, the struggle for life is more intense. She will not give up, not let go. She despises me, the cuckoo in her nest who will drain her lifeblood. I continue to return. Feed me, feed me with your so-called love. Your ghastly attention. The eyes always look-ing, always judging. Why stay? Why come to somewhere I am not wanted? Because she needs me. I serve a purpose. I love her. I am here to look after her. Sara doesn't love her. I do. I love her so much I could squeeze her to death. Suffocate her slowly. For pleasure. For I am here to teach her about love. She loves me underneath it all. When she learns to love me fully, then she can let go. And I can have my life.

I go on holiday every year. Two weeks. Torremolinos, Skiathos, Ibiza, Lanzarote. For a giggle with the girls in the bank. Sometimes on my own. I always find someone to get off with. I pretend I'm someone else. I pretend I'm a giggly girl from the bank and my eyes sparkle and I laugh and I flirt and effervesce. I become Good Fun. For two weeks. Every year. A holiday. Then I come home to Mum. I like traveling.

Something with Fish

SANDA PERLMAN

(Mrs. Anna Warren has come to the vet's office to give Miss Kitty away while her husband is dying.)

ANNA: I'll just stand here if you don't mind. Stand here and hold Miss Kitty who's never been away from home in all the years we've had her and that's almost thirteen if you count this week which we shouldn't. The Mister and me want to thank you for finding her a new home since everyone we asked wanted a kitten since they're so cute. The Mister told them they might not end up cute but if you took Miss Kitty you'd know what you were getting right away. And if you feed her good she could be around a long time.

Did you say these people had children, or was it just like the Mister and me who always wanted them? The Mister thought it was because he was so much older, but I read once that a man had a baby when he was nearly ninety-nine, and his wife was twenty-two which is even younger than me. I know personally that Kitty would love to have some children to play with. Sometimes it happens like that. You grow up and all you want is a little place to live and some land to plant your own tomatoes, since the ones in the stores taste like old Halloween mustaches. I loved Halloween but if you don't have children, people think you're crazy dressing up and hanging black cats in your window. If anyone made fun of your clothes you could just say, "This is my Halloween costume, thank you," because Mama made me promise to be polite no matter how nasty those children got to be. One time Mama took my school picture and pasted it on a cardboard playing card she'd drawn so good I looked just like the Queen of Hearts.

Everyone called me "Queenie" all day long and I was third runner-up in the costume parade which is the best I ever did at anything. *(Pause)*

Did you say this couple had a house 'cause Kitty's used to one room and the bath down the hall so anything more will seem like a palace which she would just love. I can't seem to remember a thing you told me after I said the Mister would be staying at the hospital permanent.

My father taught me to play cards in the hospital. Fish and War and that other game you play by yourself. We were visiting Mama who lost her leg from her sugar being so bad. She cried when they told her they were taking it off since she said her only pleasures in life were her Hershey kisses, dancing with my father at the Legion Hall on Friday nights, and having me of course. Kitty loves candy too but it's the treats that taste like chicken or fish which are her favorite. Mama said each of us has a special weakness and God will forgive us if we ask just once. The Mister's weakness is cigarettes which saved his life once in the army when he bent over to light up and a bullet whizzed right by his butt. Guess you only get saved once though. Not like Miss Kitty who must surely have more than nine lives.

When I met the Mister he was bigger than me and stronger too. Now I can almost pick him up in my arms. You're sure there's no children at this new house Kitty's going to? I keep forgetting. Daddy said he had to tell me important things five times. Like when he said Mama was dead. I was thirteen and kept falling asleep before he could finish. They wouldn't let me see her or the leg but I cried so hard they finally let me in. There was me and Mama and the light from Jesus beaming right down on her like something from a movie. She looked like a bride in that white gown and Daddy said that was right since she was now the bride of Jesus and all the angels would be at their wedding. He wasn't jealous at all. I thought that was nice 'til Daddy died and then my head hurt wondering if Jesus could marry him too. So I just stopped thinking about heaven 'til last week when they said the Mister probably wouldn't be coming home again and how I should consider my "options." I keep trying to figure out what they want me to say, but all I can see is the Mister's skin falling off his bones and me alone. That's when I made up my mind I wasn't leaving the Mister again 'cause I left Daddy in mine shaft 34 and I still dream of him trying to get out. The Mister worked right near Daddy in number 34, but he had a toothache so bad that day they had to pull it. He come as soon as he heard there was an accident and stood right next to me 'til they told us they were shutting it up for good. When the fellow from the news stuck that camera in my face and asked me how I felt being all alone, the Mister said, "Bert's kid don't answer dumb questions" and took me right home. Made me Campbell's tomato soup and a grilled American cheese just like Daddy, then put me to sleep in my bed and sat up in the living room chair all night so I wouldn't be lonely. We been together ever since and he always says it's a privilege to be doing things for a woman like me. I believe him too, 'cause he's always been a gentleman in every way and even clips my toenails.

You didn't say there were children, did you? No, I remember and you won't have to say another word. But would you tell those people Kitty never grabs food from the table and she's a real good mouser which I personally consider a gift. The Mister says maybe Kitty has been better for us than children since you never know how children will turn out, or if they'll turn on you when you're not looking like his own boy did. I said you can never know what God is sending you, like meeting the Mister the same day I lost Daddy.

I forgot to give you this, which reminds me to tell the people taking Kitty it would be real nice if they gave her a special treat once a week. Not that she's picky 'cause she'll eat whatever you give her. It's a small weakness really to have a treat. Just a little something with fish would be just fine.

Fruct

VIVIENNE PLUMB

(Sharyn hangs up the phone. She stays sitting in her chair. After a second, she cries a little. She wipes her eyes and addresses Mr. Square Eyes. Throughout this speech, Mr. Square Eyes, the TV, could also react by going on or off, changing channels, or turning to white-out fuzz.)

SHARYN: Let me tell ya, Mr. Square Eyes, it's easier ta be a telly than a human.

If yer a telly then I guess yer pretty well know what yer goin ta be doin for the resta yer life. It's totally sweet. Yer just "on" or "off," switchin channels, a bitta fine tunin if yer feel a bit squiggly, and chuck in some volume. But bein a human is far more complicated.

Of course I wanna do somethin, but I don't wanna do none of them borin things that Mum and Mrs. Dowd and Mr. Spitzoni and Karyn all tell me ta do. That's all stuff ta do with them, not me. Sharyn. *(By now, Sharyn is kneeling on the stage in front of Mr. Square Eyes.)* What I really want is ta have it full on, I want it piled up, not dribbled out ta me. I mean you're only a telly, so I guess it's hard fer you ta understand, but even you get overheated sometimes, right?

I wanna be a fully certified totally qualified and paid up member of the Pile High Club. I want it all like the telly ads, an I'm waitin here fer it ta start happenin.

(Really getting into it) Look, I see life as a cheese sandwich, an let me tell you, I wanna big bite. I want it comin at me, I want the bread, the butter, the fillin, and the crust. The whole thing. An I bin waitin, let me tell you.

(Quieter) When I watch you late at night, Mr. Square

Eyes, yer've immersed yerself in yer own light. It blinks and shifts and flickers and changes, and sometimes I imagine the light fallin like that on me, lightin up me own little corner. Some illumination. I know it'll happen, I can feel it comin.

Ruth

LINDSAY PRICE

(Ruth, a single woman in her forties, is fighting breast cancer. She is recalling a dream.)

RUTH: I am on the bus, returning home from the hospital. It's right after the operation. As soon as I woke up, they handed me my clothes and pointed out the nearest bus stop. You're done! Good-bye! Don't forget to write!

My shirt is all hills and valleys. Earth clinging to the rocks, skin taut to the bone. Curving down into the shadow of my chest. I didn't agree to this. I didn't agree. They took it without my permission. Tricked me, drugged me. *(Speaking directly to a another bus passenger)* "Stop staring at me!" The people on the bus are staring at the hills and valleys of my chest. Pointing at the flat spaces. "Haven't you ever seen an Amazon before! I am an Amazon. Fit for Battle! Scared and Sacred! Shield close to my chest like a second skin, sword stretching out, an extension of my fingers. *(She lets out a battle cry.)* You can stare all you want! I'm in control. I'm in control!"

Suddenly, I can feel movement underneath my shirt. I take a peek inside to see that the valleys have gone. It's not my chest anymore, it's a vast hole which begins to breathe of its own volition. *(Speaking to a passenger)* "Can I borrow your newspaper? You're not reading it. You haven't touched it for ten blocks! I have a black hole under my shirt. Thank you. Thank you." I bury myself in the classifieds, trying to hide my entire torso. My chest breathes in and sucks the newspaper inside. My shirt is next and I'm sitting on the bus, topless: one mound of flesh, one black hole. *(To the bus passengers)* "Stop staring at me!" Everything on the bus is being pulled towards me, drawn towards my chest. A baby, the bus driver, the bus itself. *(Talking to the passengers)* "I'm sorry. I'm so sorry. I'd help you if I could."

But I can't. I can't stop the pull, can't stop the life being sucked through my chest. The street signs, the street, the city, the people, the deserts, the oceans, the earth, the stars, the universe. I am all alone. Topless. One mound of flesh. One black hole. There's nothing around me. No people. No deserts. No oceans.

(Calling out) Hello? Anybody there? Hello? You'd think the dream would be over, by now. You'd think I'd wake up. But I don't. I don't. *(Singsong voice)* Ruth Doyle is alive and well. She doesn't drink whisky and she knows how to spell. Ruth Doyle is alive and well.

The Road

SUSANNA RALLI

(The speaker is a woman in her thirties. She wanders onstage in a daze, searching for the grave of her dead child, who was killed by a hit-and-run driver. Suddenly, somewhat to her surprise, she finds herself by the grave. She kneels and picks off some dead flowers and weeds. Then she stands and speaks, partly to the child, and partly to herself.)

A strange thing has happened since you left, my dear. I don't see cars anymore. I see shapes and colors, but it doesn't register that they might hit me. Or hurt me. I look for the busiest road I can find, and I step out, walk right out in the middle of the traffic. (She steps forward, as if into traffic.) I don't look both ways, as I was taught to do. I walk right out into the street, feeling the breeze of the cars going by me so close. But then a strange thing happens. It's as if God, who has been so absent lately, suddenly looks down and says, "Oh dear, look at that woman. She's in danger. I must save her." And, somehow, I find myself on the other side of the road. Untouched. And even then, after such a miracle, I don't see anything. (Pause. She glances at the ground.) But sometimes, when I can't stand it anymore, I do see something. I see you, all alone, walking across an empty road. And a car coming out of nowhere. And I ask, "Why wasn't God watching then?" But then it passes. (She stares straight ahead, into the distance.)

Perfection

DEANNA RILEY

(Roxy, a middle-class woman, notices someone staring at her.)

ROXY: I am perfect. I know what you're thinking. . . . But you're wrong. I'm right. Don't worry. Happens all the time. Despite what most people think, you're not born perfect. Born with a silver spoon, born on third base, born again, but not born perfect. I was making myself miserable. Everywhere I looked, I was wrong. Wasn't thin enough, tan enough, sexy enough, smart enough, dumb enough. Miserable. Miserable. Miserable. Couldn't cook, clean, or macrame holiday placemats. Couldn't balance a checkbook or do math homework. My doctors were out of network, my cell phone was out of range, and my computer was out of disk space. My grocery line was the longest, my ATM was jammed, and my dog had fleas. Again. My Christmas cards were never addressed, written, or mailed. But I did buy the cards. My favorite ice cream is vanilla. Plain vanilla. Not even French vanilla. I was a "C" student. Sometimes I would get a "C+." Average with extra effort. The world expects extraordinary people and I was average. Not perfect. Not even a perfect failure. Average. And I wanted a change. I wanted to be on the "A-list." No waiting at crowded restaurants. Tellers open their windows just for me. Always having exact change. But how to make me change? Where to look? How to start? Then it came to me. Denial. Denial was the perfect strategy. Now I can't claim credit for it because I wasn't perfect at the time. My mother gave me the insight. My mother has always had a fabulous figure, not perfect mind you, but very good. Much better than mine to tell you the truth. Quite voluptuous. As she has gotten a little older, she has put on a few pounds and is not the size she used to be. But does she acknowledge that? Not for one second. My mother explained to me that she is wearing larger sizes because sizes were originally designed around 1906 and American women were smaller then. As advances in medicine, diet, and exercise have progressed, American women have grown in size. So the fashion designers all over the world got together to make adjustments in sizes. Although she "wears" a fourteen or sixteen, she "is" still a size six. The sizes got smaller and it's all because of the fashion designers' international conspiracy. My mother is a very happy woman. She believes she is the same size she was when she was twenty-two. Ignorance is bliss. Denial is the way to happiness. At first, I had a little trouble working in the denial. At the bank, I cut in front of a six-foot-two, 210-pound woman. Lesson one: Pick your denials carefully. The next time, I pictured myself in the front of the line and everyone in front of me was performance art. Very entertaining. No stress. They actually paid me to see the performance. What more could I want? Then the perfection started rolling. My steaks were actually cooked medium rare and not something in between. The ATM gave me an extra twenty. Got the cheapest long distance coverage. Bought placemats. Balanced my checkbook. Got a raise. Got two. Had groceries delivered at home. Won a new computer. Dumped my old cell phone. My dog's fleas left for him for another dog. Felt taller, thinner, sexier. And I started wearing pre-fashion-conspiracy sizes. Vanilla was the flavor of the week—for a month. Finally, I had achieved perfection. Bliss. There's only one impediment to total worldwide perfection. I need you to help acknowledge that I'm perfect. "Duchess of Perfection. Queen of Denial." *(Raises voice)* While I reign supreme, everyone will be happy. Perfection in every pot. Denial at every door. "Queen for a Day every day." What a success story. A "C" is an "A" in every way. Help me show others how to use this gift. Ignorance is bliss. And everyone wants to be happy. How can you deny me? I'm perfect.

Clue Phone

ROBIN ROTHSTEIN

(Wendy, in her thirties, is seated on one end of a couch hold-ing a glass of red wine. There is an end table next to her with an open bottle and a phone. She drinks.)

WENDY: Okay, time to be frank. You're right. There is some-thing going on with me. I really didn't want to say anything yet, but since you're being so persistent. *(Pause. Smiles.)* I have been seeing the world's greatest guy! Aaaaaaaaaah! I've said it! Well, it hasn't been that long and I wasn't sure if it was going to stick. I know. Can you believe it? His name is Tim. I mean Timothy. Timothy, Timothy, Timothy. In fact, I expect him to call soon so we can make plans for tonight. Yup. Well, you know what they say, "It's when you're *not* looking." Well, it's only been a few weeks, so I don't like consider us "official," but I'm glad I can finally tell someone I'm so about to bust out of my control tops! And I have this feeling . . . I think he could be "the one"! Aaaaaaaaaah! I know! Isn't it crazy? Me. "The General Cho's Chicken Eating No Social Life Video Renting Misfit!" Can you believe it? I feel so blessed. So blessed. He's smart, funny . . . well, I mean . . . in his own way funny. Not laugh out loud hilari-ous split a gut and accidentally fart funny, more like a . . . beige funny. You know. Like droll? He's actually kind of quiet. But I've discovered that I prefer quiet people. I do. I am actually a quiet person. Whenever I talk, it's just a facade. *(Long pause. Wendy sips more wine and glances at the phone.)* The greatest thing about Tim—Timothy—is that he's not creative. He's an accountant. I know, can you believe it? Not to say that he's *boring*. I mean, he doesn't say much, but when he does speak, he's very sensual. He has this way of saying "refund" that makes me want to stick my tongue right down his throat. He also has that kind of great pedigree that my mother always dreamed about. The kind that could get you into the *New York Times* bridal announcements? Last name Twitmeyer, undergrad Princeton, mother a descendant of Kierkegaard. And to top it all off, he's normal. Yes. Can you believe it? I finally found a normal person. Hoo-FUCKING-ray! And a gentleman, can I tell you? He almost always pays. I make that false attempt to pay my share, you know the hand going towards the pocketbook motion, but he almost always stops me. *(Pause)* Oh . . . well . . . the sex . . . it's . . . let's just say, "Heaven" is an understatement. *(She drinks some wine.)* Except he has these two cats. They always start crawling on my back right when I start giving him a blow job. Talk about your "ménage à cattre." *(She laughs hysterically at this. Then slowly, her laughter dies. Plainly.)* The first time we slept together, Timothy was pumping me hard for, well, a while and I started worrying that I wasn't going to be able to come and the more I worried the worse, well, you know. So, he's pumping and grunting and murmuring and I'm trying to make myself excited by fantasizing that I'm this new girl on the job in a porn video being bonked by her dirty old boss when all of a sudden I get this soft, wet feeling in my ear. Ohmygod. It was soooooo erotic. I *exploded*. I *swear*. I had the most mammoth orgasm I have ever had. Yeah, I know. Isn't that great! I was really happy to know it could happen for me. The only thing *is* . . . *(She starts laughing.)* . . . Now this is really funny . . . I'm not sure if what I felt in my ear was Timothy, or one of the cats. *(She drinks more wine.)* What it comes right down to? Is that it's comfortable when we're together. And that's what's really important. I mean, I'm not like *instantly* attracted to him. My clit doesn't perk up and scream gimme gimme whenever I think about him, or when he touches me, but because we were friends first, it's like we care about one another. I, you know, eventually get excited. I just have to concentrate. Harder. Unless, of course, one of his cats is nearby. *(She laughs in a manic way at this and pours herself more wine. Her laugh dies. She drinks.)* So, I invited him out to a dinner celebration I threw for some friends a few days ago. We all had such a great time. He hasn't called yet to thank me for inviting him, but I'm sure it's because he's been so busy with— I think he should have called though, don't you? It's been three days. I mean it's not that important. I mean, the celebration wasn't about him, so it's not like I should really expect him to thank me. An e-mail thank you at least would have been . . . you know. *(She drinks some wine and looks at the phone.)* I've thought of calling him to see if he's OK. He was feeling a little nauseous that night. *(Pause)* It's weird, but I've been very weepy lately. I'll just spontaneously start crying and I have no idea why. Because I do feel good. Really good. I FEEL GREAT!!!! *(She looks over at the phone.)* I'm sure he must be busy at work although it's nowhere near tax season, so then *why God haven't you fucking called me! Huh?* What is it? I'm not *perfect* enough? I'm not in your league? Not up to the Twitmeyer standard? Is that it? Well, you know what, Timothy? Tim? *(Short pause)* Up yours. That's right. Up yours you cheap-assed, socially dysfunctional cat-worshipping freak! You're not in *my* league, OK? You're not in *my* league. So you can just, you know, how dare you not fucking call me in three days! How dare you. You know, I don't even fucking like you! You can't diss somebody who doesn't like you! It doesn't work that way! I'm supposed to diss *you!* *(She starts strangling the phone.)* THIS IS NOT THE WAY IT'S SUPPOSED TO WORK! I'M SUPPOSED TO DISS YOU GODDAMNIT! I'M SUPPOSED TO DISS YOU! *(She is about to hurl the phone across the room but stops just as she's about to let go. She looks at the phone for a moment, composes herself, then picks up the receiver and dials. She waits a few moments until someone picks up on the other end.)* Hello Tim? It's Wendy. *(Short pause)*

Yeah. Listen, I just wanted to—*(Pause)* Yeah well . . . *(Pause)*
I've been really busy too, so—*(Pause)* Uhhhh . . . *(Pause)*
Indian's . . . great. *(Pause)* Sound's good. *(Pause)* Me too.
(Pause) See you soon. *(She hangs up and picks up her glass of wine.)* I knew he'd call.

Cigarette
(from Bleach)

LEAH RYAN

(Julie, in her late twenties, is contemplating a visit to her family.)

JULIE: I lie in bed and I smoke a cigarette and I try to get up and I smoke another cigarette and I still can't get up so I smoke another cigarette. The shades are drawn, the clock says seven-thirty, I have no idea what that means, which is not a good sign, I think, so I smoke another cigarette. I know there's a train I should be on, I don't have any clean clothes, I have to go to the bank, I need to get more cigarettes, I need to dye my hair again, I can't deal with all this so I smoke another cigarette. I think about me, myself, dressed, clean, ready to go to the train station, I see myself carrying a bag, an overnight bag, maybe it's afternoon, maybe it's evening, I've already put in a day's work and I have done my laundry and so I deserve a cigarette. I see myself on the train, it's a commuter train, you can't smoke, it's a short distance, but I still want a cigarette. When I get to Grand Central I get out and have a cigarette, stand on the street, people are coming at me like bullets, I really feel like going to a bar, but then I go into the subway. I'll arrive full of cravings, I'll smell the food cooking that I don't have any appetite for, I'll want to say where's the booze, but I'll be civilized, I'll drink a glass of wine, or two, or seven, and I'll smoke on the fire escape, which is what my mother does, and my mother will frown at me because I have no good news and I don't look well, I know I don't. So who the hell do I think I am? If I took three bottles of wine and a carton of cigarettes out to the fire escape I still wouldn't feel right, I'd still feel like I was falling off a cliff, and even if I did that, it would be wrong, because that's no way to visit your family. So I just lie there and smoke, and think . . . all I have to do is put some clothes on, any old clothes, and walk three blocks to the bar. That's all. I will. Right after this cigarette.

Little Red Riding Hood's Mother

TAMMY RYAN

(Joan has moved to the country with her daughter, and has just learned that girls in the area are being abducted at the school bus stops.)

JOAN: This is what I want to know: how come we never hear the story about Little Red Riding Hood's Mother? What about her side of it? Standing on the doorstep, watching Little Red as she disappears round the bend into the dark woods. Heart beating, hands wringing, hyperventilating, completely powerless, frozen on that doorstep. What the hell was the matter with her? Letting her defenseless child walk through the woods by herself with a maniac wolf on the loose? She knew full well that forest was full of wolves, but she sent her out there with a basketful of bait! "Stay on the path," like that's gonna save her. It's almost like she wanted little Red out of the way. . . . Maybe she couldn't stand the pressure of living in the woods anymore, the isolation, doing nothing but baking cookies for her sick mother. And you never hear about that relationship. Why doesn't she visit her sick mother herself? And where was Little Red's father? No one ever addresses that. And what about the Woodcutter? A strange man in the woods with an ax. Why does everyone automatically trust him? It's a frightening story.

Thrown by Angels

GWENDOLYN SCHWINKE

(Jane Doe, a married woman, speaks to the audience.)

JANE: I been told I'm stubborn. By my husband. My husband says I'm the most stubborn woman on God's Green Earth. Just like that he says it. "You Are The Most Stubborn Woman On God's Green Earth." All the time: "The Most Stubborn Woman on God's Green Earth." Gets my back up.

So one day I said, you know the earth isn't green, you know. There's a lot of it that's not anywhere close to green: Deserts—brown. Polar ice caps—white, all white. Oceans. Three-fourths of the world is covered with oceans, everybody knows that, and oceans are blue. "Well, actually, they're kinda green," he says. I say blue. I was watching one of those science programs once on TV and they kept calling it the Blue Planet. Maybe that's the way God sees it too. Maybe it's God's Blue Earth . . .

Maybe God sees things completely differently. Maybe God sees all darkness with little red and yellow lights where there's people and animals and things, like in that movie, *Predator*, where the monster could only see body heat or something. And my husband says, "Are you comparing God to a monster in a movie with Arnold Schwarzenegger? Because, first off," he says, "that's blasphemy, God is not a monster, and second, in that movie, they get the monster in the end and I'm sure if He wanted to, God could kick Arnold Schwarzenegger's butt."

I say, that's not what I'm saying. You're completely missing the point. All I'm saying is: God's Green Earth is not necessarily Green. You might be wrong about that. And if you're wrong about that, you might be wrong about me being The Most Stubborn Woman On It.

And he just looks at me and then says, like he's on one of those lawyer shows or something, he says, "I rest my case."

He might have a point.

I'd never tell him that, of course. But it's true. Once I get an idea in my head, it's hard for me to let it go; I'm like a dog with a bone. Especially when the person I'm talking to is not getting my point. They don't have to agree with me, they just have to listen. Listen and get it. And if they don't, I can't let it go, I set my jaw. You know, somebody in the Bible kills somebody else with a jawbone. If my husband was here, he'd remind you that it was the jawbone of an ass, actually, but that's another point. The point is the jaw is really strong. I heard somewhere that the muscles in the jaw are the strongest muscles—per size, you know—in the human body. And it's because way, way back we had to use our jaws, you know, life or death.

For instance, say you're living in the jungle, or in the savannah, or wherever, you have to eat. And let's say you have a family, you have to feed your family. Now say you and your family haven't eaten good for a week. And you finally catch a . . . a . . . an animal, a wild pig, say. And you got it in your trap or you hit it with a rock or whatever, and you go to get it in your hands and it's not dead yet. You're holding it and it's trying to get away, and if it does you're not going to eat, and your family's not going to eat and what are you going to do? Use your jaw. Clamp down on that thing for dear life, and don't let it go. Survival.

That's why our jaws are so strong. Survival. And if you ask me, stubbornness is like that too. It's good for something, is all I'm saying.

(She touches the sides of her face.) Sometimes I hear a ringing sound in my ears—and I get dizzy. Like it's just me holding on. God's Green Earth (or whatever color we're gonna say that it is) spinning around for all it's worth, and me just clamped down, holding on for dear life.

Excerpt from *Labor Pains, A Comedy in Nine Months*

LISA DIANA SHAPIRO

(Jake, a pregnant woman in her thirties, talks to her unborn child.)

JAKE: Okay, we gotta have a talk. Now, I realize that I don't know you at all yet, and I'm probably making assumptions about you I have no business making. But bear with me. Well, I guess you don't have much choice about that, do you?

That's sort of my point, actually—you don't have much choice about anything right now. I mean, your decision-making processes are years in the future. And I thought I could wait, but it seems I'm going to make certain decisions for you. And if I'm wrong, you'll grow up to be in therapy your entire life, you'll go to weekly meetings of groups called Adult Children of Overbearing Jewish Mothers, you'll write a horrible book about me and you'll make a lot of money—I guess that's not so bad. I feel like I have your entire future in my hands. My god, if I toilet train you too early you could grow up to be a Republican. I gotta read some more books about this stuff.

What I'm trying to say is, I think I want you to be Jewish. I tried, I really did, to be open-minded about it. I want you to be your own person, not just a reflection on me. But I can't just let you do a little Esther Williams baptism routine and pretend it means nothing to me.

There are certain things I want to give you—rituals and stories and songs, the things that shaped my life, and my mother's, and her mother's, all the way back to the shtetl. I guess I want to give you your history.

And if by chance, when you die—*(She spits through her fingers.)* Oh, god, I'm turning into my grandmother—if you find out that Jesus Christ really is the messiah—and, like, he doesn't want to redeem you 'cause you haven't been baptized—tell him it's my fault. Okay? I'm sure he'll make an exception for you. After all, he was a nice Jewish boy.

A Teenager's Guide to the Universe

JUDY SHEEHAN

(Allison is a college student, studying for her art history final exam. She pauses to address the audience.)

ALLISON: Ancient Egyptians believed in reincarnation. So do lots of people today, but the Egyptians had a very specific Reincarnation Plan. You die, your body is cleaned out and wrapped up and put away, and then one day you wake up in a whole new place. And it's important to wake up with all the stuff you're going to need. Money, jewelry. Stuff. But we've opened the tombs, and really—the mummies are not going to wake up. The Egyptians were wrong. . . . *(Pause)* Well. At least, I think they were wrong. I'm pretty sure. But then again—who knows? Maybe they could still turn out to be right someday. Maybe the Museum of Natural History is crawling with mummies right this very second, and they're all wondering, "Where the hell am I and where is my jewelry?" Or maybe that'll happen next week. I doubt it, but I'm starting to realize that it's impossible to be certain about *anything* anymore. Everything changes. The earth is shifting beneath our feet. Hey, I thought I was going to marry Jimmy. And now I'm not. I was wrong. I'm okay with that. Or . . . I will be. I had to break up with him. You see, I had this dream. I dreamt that I was having sex with Dr. Asher. And when I woke up, I thought—this is sort of like cheating on Jimmy. And then I realized that I didn't mind cheating on Jimmy. In fact, I wanted to cheat on Jimmy. I am all for cheating on Jimmy. I hate the way he eats, I resent the way he brushes his teeth, and when he tries to speak Italian I want to choke him with my hands. But this is all petty stuff, right? You don't trash your future over that. Do you? Well. I do. I did. And now the future is uncertain. Maybe I'll wake up in the Land of the Dead with all my jewelry. And maybe I'll wake up alone, dreaming about sex with professors. I just don't know. Sorry.

Wild Fire
(from *Epiphanies*)

LILLIAN ANN SLUGOCKI

(Cybele is seventeen years old. She has been asked to give a statement following her trial where she has been found guilty as an accessory to her brother's death. Her comments offstage right are addressed to her mother. The rest of the narrative is addressed to the court.)

CYBELE *(Yelling off right)*: I *said* I'd be there in a second! *(Louder)* I said I'd be there in a *second!* Are you deaf or something? For Christ's sake!

(Addressing the court) Before they take me outa here, I'm gonna have my say. I'm gonna. Nobody let me say a damn word in court, and I'm sick of people speaking for me. I got plenty of brains and I remember everything clear as day. *(Beat)* OK. We moved to this neighborhood when I was ten years old. My father left one morning, think it was summer, and he never looked back. My ma hooked up with some guy whose guts I will always hate. PLUS I never got a chance to say goodbye to my best friend, Marilyn. Marilyn's two front teeth were completely rotted away, but I still loved her anyway. I used to walk through the alley to get to her house and I called her like this: *(Singsong)* "Mar-i-lyn! Mar-i-lyn!" *(Beat)* And I am NOT the one who left behind my brother's bottle. Will you remember that? It was my ma. She did it on purpose. Said he was too old for that bottle and maybe he was and anyway that damn kid cried all night long for his damn bottle. And will you remember that it was ME who got up in the middle of the night and took him out of his crib to feed him. ME. 'Cause

frankly I couldn't stand his crying anymore— *(Beat)* And what's more this damn neighborhood was nothing but big piles of black dirt when we moved here; no trees, no grass, no nothing except a big drainage ditch where the railroad tracks used to run. And will you also remember that every damn kid in the neighborhood played in that ditch 'cause there was nothing like it anywhere on the face of this earth. *Nothing.* It was big and it was mysterious with all kinds of tunnels and hills and even a creek that gushed over in the spring when the snow melted. *(Beat)* Am I allowed to say I was lonely? That I never heard from Marilyn again? That the nuns at my new school were like big ugly birds who slapped my knuckles with big silver rulers . . . am I allowed to say the bitches made me bleed? And that my uniform made me sweat like a pig in summer and incidentally made me LOOK like a pig because who the hell can wear navy blue wool and look good? And—AND am I ALLOWED to say that my stepfather crawled into my bedroom at night on his hands and knees and nobody lifted a damn hand to save me? Can you remember all that?

(Yelling offstage) YES. Yes, it is true! IT IS! *(Beat)*

See, some kids get to play in a park or some kids got big backyards with swing sets and swimming pools, but all we had was the ditch and that was fine. Even when the cabbage rotted in the fields and stank up the whole neighborhood in the summer it was the closest thing to paradise I have ever known. *(Beat)* And I don't give a shit if that sounds stupid. *(Beat)* 'Cause in the summer, I collected tadpoles in jelly jars and beetles in old coffee tins and once I even caught a lizard and kept it as a pet in a yellow bucket. Fed it stale bread and dead bugs. But, the damn thing ran away from home and broke my heart. It's pretty pathetic when a runaway lizard breaks your heart—take note: last thing I want is for you to feel sorry for me. Just listen to my side of the story—that's all I ask.

(Yelling offstage) NO. I am NOT almost finished—thank you very MUCH. *(Beat)*

I knew every inch of that ditch, every mudhole, every hill,

every patch of stinkweed and rhubarb. I knew that it smelled like yellow dust and rotting cabbage in the summer, and I could close my eyes at night and listen to thousands of crickets croaking at the full moon. *(Beat)* And in the winter, when it snowed like hell, we'd drag out our sleds from the basement and slide down the hills screaming like maniacs. AND—and every kid in that neighborhood played in that ditch ESPECIALLY in the wintertime. Will you remember that? My ma said: "Young ladies shouldn't collect tadpoles and climb inside sewers on hot summer days—"

(Yelling offstage)—YOU DID! *(Beat)*

But, I didn't give a damn. I didn't wanna do what little girls were supposed to do. And I hated my new school, my new friends, and most of all I hated my new father. My REAL father who's basically forgotten I'm ALIVE used to send me postcards from around the world—like that was supposed to make me feel better or something. Shit. All I knew was that the sight of his handwriting from somewhere thousands of miles away just made me lonelier. That bastard didn't have the GUTS to look me in the eye the morning he took off and for that I will never forgive him. *(Beat)* So will you kindly remember that my heart shriveled up into a tiny ball of ice and will you remember, and this is important—that I looked real on the outside but on the inside I was fake and frozen? Huh? Will you? So—so, one morning after a really nasty night I had to get out of the house. Guess I had a bad nightmare and damn near woke up the neighborhood with my screaming and even though it was twenty below I had to get out. Will you remember the nightmare part? *(Beat)* Bet you won't. People only remember what they want— *(Beat)* Alright. Here goes. I dragged my baby brother out with me and walked to the ditch. I thought it would be cool to build a fort out of the old railroad ties—big thick pieces of wood. The sun was out but it wasn't what you'd call sunny. Too damn cold to be sunny but my brother looked real cute all wrapped up in his snowsuit—real cute. *(Beat)* We rolled the ties—or rather I did while he watched—and wrapped up like mummies, our eyes tearing from the freezing wind. I hardly noticed the damn sun slipping down the sky. I swear! PLUS we were too busy arguing to notice it had started to snow again. *(Beat)* Yeah. *(Beat)* He starting begging me to help and at first I said no but I got tired of saying no so finally I said yes. He grabbed one end and I grabbed the other and of course we slipped and that tie crashed down on our legs—pinned us like rats in a trap. *(Beat)* At first my brother cried and screamed but it didn't do no good. And hell—I thought—this ain't a bad way to die. My fingers tingled inside my mittens and my legs were numb and my nose lost all feeling, but I felt comfortable. My damn heart was frozen and soon the rest of me would be frozen as well. I looked over at my brother and his face was all red and swollen, but I thought: least he's sleeping.

(Yelling offstage) If you don't let me finish—there's MORE where this came from— *(Beat)*

When I heard those assholes coming down the street to rescue us I tried to wake up my brother—but he just flopped back and forth. Back and forth. And he wouldn't open his damn eyes no matter what I did. I even slapped him—but not to hurt him—I swear! Will you remember that? *(Beat)* After we buried him I went back to the old neighborhood to see if I could find his bottle. And the whole damn place had changed—for one thing our house had been moved—now it was a parking lot. I couldn't find Marilyn and I couldn't find that damn bottle. But I want him and YOU to know I tried. Will you remember that? Will you? *(Beat)* OK. I'm finished. I'm ready to go. I SAID I'm ready to go.

Hanging Women

DONNA SPECTOR

(Celandine, 30, speaks to her mother and sister in the living room of their shabby house in the country. She climbs on a chair, clutching a radio, which plays Mozart softly.)

CELANDINE: I don't need men anymore. I did, I admit, spend years looking for my perfect mate. The dark side who would let me see my bright side. And the other way around, like a two-way mirror. I wanted someone staring in my eyes, not in an unnerving way, but showing me he listens, he *appreciates* who I am. Someone to cook with, not chicken, but lobster thermidor, steak tartare, asparagus quiche. He holding the bowl and I the spoon, in perfect synchronicity. Someone who loves to hear me read Edna St. Vincent Millay by wine-laced candlelight on Saturday nights. Who will read me Wallace Stevens over coffee and oranges Sunday mornings. Someone for whom I could buy silk underwear and paint my toenails silver. Even shave my legs—they have gotten so hairy! A fire builder, a door holder, who doesn't condemn me for reading *Cosmopolitan* as well as *The New Yorker*. Someone who will riffle the hairs at the back of my neck, nibble my earlobe in elevators, who will hold me, because my body is so lonely, it has forgotten the human touch.

But now I understand these are adolescent fantasies. I don't need a man wrapped around me in bed, warming the sheets on freezing nights. And I am perfectly content to eat, not chicken, but a single artichoke and an isolated glass of wine. I like to open doors, fires are clichéd, poetry does not need to be shared, and I adore cotton underpants that make me look like a female wrestler. So I have no pressed flowers in

136

fading photo albums. What if I get no love letters in blue envelopes and the phone stays silent and black. Why have a color phone when there is no man in your life? What do I care? I shall never have a broken heart or a vaginal infection. Men always disappoint you, and I choose to be disappointed with no one but myself. There is such freedom in this decision. I am finally an adult, responsible for my own existence. *(She opens her arms wide.)* I embrace the status quo, and I shall die, unremittingly alone, in an old, rotting house by the sea!

Men & Cars

DIANE SPODAREK

(The present. Twilight. The Last Exit Bar. Maggie is a single mother, a musician, and a temp from Detroit who lives in Manhattan.)

MAGGIE: I like to drink a tall Bud when I'm walking around the streets of Manhattan. I keep it in a brown paper bag and sip it through a straw. Sometimes I like to stand on the corner and wait. Wait for the men. You ever watch men and their cars? Ever watch men look *under* their cars? I like the way men look when they look under their cars.

I like to watch men sit in their cars, start them up, find out they don't start, get out, look at the car, then go to the hood. Open the hood, look in, go back to the inside of the car, and try to start it up again. Get out again, look under the car, look at the ground, look at the spill on the ground, look all around, sometimes at their companion, if they're with someone. If not, look for another man in the vicinity to share this moment. Then there are two or three sometimes four men looking under the hood or looking under the car, or at the ground. Sometimes they stare at the spill on the ground together, and then they look at each other and they get that look. I like that look. It's somehow familiar. I can't put my finger on it, I can't really say what it is, but it just gives me a funny feeling watching them, the men and their cars, although I don't really think it has anything to do with the fact that I'm from Detroit.

Bounty

CARIDAD SVICH

(A compartment on a train. Coral is revealed. She is an elderly woman with a youthful countenance. She wears a satin-and-lace dress and long pearls. Around her neck hangs a small velvet bag.)

CORAL: Nineteen hundred and twenty-nine.
That's when I came here from Santiago in Chile.
It was another kind of land then.
The fields gave you a sense of peace.

I was a spit of five.
Straight off the boat to New York,
and the stink of cabbage and fresh fruit.
And in the air a sorrowful blues.
There was a woman named Bessie who walked down my
    street
with a rope of pearls 'round her neck
and the finest feathers in her hair:
coq rouge, marabou, and ostrich.
She had a voice like thunder.
She'd say, "My name is Miss Smith
and don't you dare forget it."
She was strange. So different from the women in Chile.
And she carried herself in such a way
as to say, "It does not matter what anyone thinks of me.
I do as I please."

Here I was. A girl of five. Come all the way from Santiago.
Didn't know a thing. Could hardly say my name.

Coral. Fool name for a child. Cursed name for an old woman.
Can never live up to it. Will always smell death in it.
Who wants to know they've been named after a skeleton
of small animals?

Oh, but Miss Smith . . .
she walked down the street without a care,
wrapping her strong laugh
'round tender young men and tall, wide-hipped women
with the smell of marigolds in their hair.
I thought, "I may not know much,
but I know that's what I want.
That's the kind of woman I want to be.
Someone who belongs to everyone and no one.
A self-made, self-possessed bird with the taste
of poison on her lips."

It wasn't until years later, when I was an awkward thirteen,
and living scrabble-ass poor in the lower side of the city
with some second cousins who had taken me in after my
    father
died, that I read in the back of the newspaper,
in a column no more than two inches long,
that one Bessie Smith had died in a little room
in Mississippi, far away from New York and my side of the
street, and farther away from my Santiago and all it had
meant to me.

Of course, the first thing I did was go to St. Louis
when I got the chance. I wanted to see the place that
she'd named the blues for.
I found myself in a whole world of bent rivers.
Right smack on the heels of Prohibition's repeal.
Now, what is a shy girl of thirteen with a fool name
like Coral going to do in a town busting open
with liquor and industry, when all she's got

is a crooked smile and a couple of dollars slipped
into her brassiere?

Whore. Yes.
Problem was, I wasn't much good at it.
I spent more on soap than what I made in a week.
I couldn't stand any other soap but Maja from Spain,
and they don't just sell that on the street.
Not in St. Louis. You got to order that through
the catalogue, get it sent down from New York.
Pretty soon, I couldn't live on the cheap.
I was a no-good woman, half a child,
stuck in St. Louis, and damn Spanish to boot.
That's what they called me. "The Spanish bit."
I kept saying, "I'm from Chile. South America."
No one knew what I meant.

(Coral looks out window.)
Miles of countryside. Miles and miles . . .
You'll get sick of it after a while: bounty.
You'll start to hunger for stripped skies and leveled
smoke, and a place to hang your bloody torso.
'Cause that's how it will get after a while,
after days and days of splitting work:
bloody and broken and filled with crushed charcoal.

You think corn just grows without anybody tending to it,
without anybody breaking their back over the husks
and the leaves and the making of the meal?
You'll get so you can't stand the sight of beauty.

You'll start throwing sulfur on the roses
and watch them die.
And in the hollow of evening
you'll wait for a rumor of grass,
so you can unfence the cancer wrought over this land.

And you'll pray for the cancer to spread
And infect everything:
The corn, the insects, the trains of milk and syrup,
And the sailors, drunk on oil from the rotten sea.
And when you read the paper in the morning,
you'll expect your prayers to have been answered
but all you will see is more of everything.
Endless bounty.

And you'll know that your lovers will remain photographs
on a wall, in a breast pocket, in the inside of your seam,
and the train will go on past origins and history,
and the moon will go unburied.
And Christ's children will sail
on tiny rafts of twigs burning in the sea,
and they will come here,
like you, like me,
and place their faith in a brilliant fever of a dream
because they have spent their lives trembling,
their days in want,
and it is bounty that they seek,
the very bounty that is killing me.

Two Sides to Every Story

MARY E. WEEMS

(The stage is set with a white wooden cross splattered with blood. A 1990s Mary walks out wearing an African caftan and carrying a white industrial bucket filled with water. She washes the cross down, sits on the edge of the stage and begins.)

MARY: Seem like everybody I know's name is Mary. At work I spend all day tipping my head right and left listening to "Mary" this and "Mary" that. *(Pause)* There's three Marys on my floor, and I'm the only black one—but of course nowadays "hey nigger" wouldn't be polite and nobody has the nerve to call me black Mary—so as usual, my color is *not* a plus. *(She starts humming.)* "Mary had a little lamb, little lamb, little lamb—" *(Starts chuckling)* Ever thought about why there's so many dumb songs about Marys? What do you think would happen if a '90s Mary went to the hospital and delivered a lamb? Talk about cloning—churches all over the world would be examining their bibles for an explanation for something that's unexplainable! *(Gets up and starts decorating the cross with the sign for woman. She has several of them in the pockets of her garment and they stick with a little pressure.)* Speaking of explaining, I wish someone would tell me what really happened between my sistah Mary and her husband when he couldn't find a room. *(Pause)* I heard an old African proverb one time that said if the lion wrote the story instead of the hunter—everything would change—and *(quietly)* between you, me, and the Marys I think if we heard her story, the line between state and religion would cross and the space would be red. I don't know why, but I think about sistah Mary a lot. What was she really like? *(Pause)* I bet she was hot for her day, probably said "motherfucka" and everything. Did she dance? Get mad at Joe? Insist on going out to dinner on her birthday—sneak and smoke late at night *(pause)* wear makeup—I can't make up my mind but one thing I do know—she definitely wasn't white and she wasn't a virgin either. Sometime when it's quiet like it is now I imagine her here—making crosses for a living—nailing each one to a different street corner, whitewashing it—washing it, washing it over and over like she's trying to erase the old story from everywhere—like if she does she'll get to come back—and be and say no—No like we supposed to be able to do now—doesn't matter if we sleepin' with, shackin', married, divorced, or just meetin' for the first time NO IS NO—period. *(Pause)* How do you tell God no? I mean if it's a high-powered fuck—how do you stop it? Suppose you don't want to give birth to a sweet, ever-loving sin eater? What if you want to stick with your vows—shun adultery? Stay away from temptation? I mean maybe Mary said, "HELL NO" loud and clear, but God thought she was only talking to Lucifer? I mean, you see what I mean—these what-ifs start adding up and all of a sudden—his story starts sounding like a cover-up. Now, personally I know all about cover-ups—Here at the cross plant we're experts at it—spend our days and sometime half the night traveling the world, being Marys *(pause)* washing the crosses that carry *(pause)* her blood.

Tripp

ERIN CRESSIDA WILSON

(A "post-feminist" young intern speaks her mind in a controlled, friendly, sensual manner.)

YOUNG WOMAN: My vagina is not your soap box. My vagina is not a place that you can claim to be sporting feminist values. My vagina is a talking mouth of petals and it has something to say, and it goes something like this:

I'm looking for empowering and positive images of heterosexual sex. I'm coming out as a heterosexual woman. I'm coming out as a woman who refuses to surrender to the rash of sex suits that has overtaken our nation.

Gloria Steinem, various seventies feminists, why did you get laryngitis the week the Clinton witch hunt began? Because you are the ones that gave me the power to wear garter belts and lingerie. I am a sexy twenty-something-year-old, and if I want to blow the president, I will, and if he wants to be blown, he will, and I thank God that the president of these United States is blow-*able*.

Because Sister, Sister, my vagina is not your soap box. It is not a political orifice. It is a part of me, not separate. Don't *further* separate my sexuality in the name of sisterhood. I think fucking my boss is my prerogative. I think fucking our President should become a requirement of the White House Internship Program, in fact I think knee pads should be issued to all subordinates in every office throughout America. Because I am the new young woman and this is where I excel.

Oh, I see, you're jealous. Of me? Of him? Maybe you wish I would go down on *you*, Linda Tripp.

By the way, my vagina is not your cash machine, either. If

I want to climb on top of President Clinton's face, have him tongue me silly, so be it. Because I'm tight and delirious baby, and you are loose and dry. Tried estrogen pills?

My vagina is not your soap box. It is not yours. It is not "ours," "we" women. And you are not my sister.

And as for myself, I wouldn't want your stanky slash as my soapbox. I'll take your tackiness, I'll step right on top of your tackiness and say: I know the intricacies of President Clinton's prick, I know just how far down my throat he likes it to time with his shot into me. And you better believe I love the feeling of his spunk falling over my taste buds, running down my chin, and down my throat. And that is why I got the smile that all of America is seeing. Because my lips and teeth are sparkling with his anointment.

Suicide

Y YORK

(Sylvia, 20, advises another patient.)

You screw it up you don't get a second chance. Nobody trusts you. Doesn't matter what you say, you say, "Listen, I'm not going to do it again." You say, "Listen. I'm not. Going to do it. Again." You can say, "No, no. My life is really worth living; I'd never do it again." That is if you can say that without gagging. Doesn't matter. They don't trust you. They say they do, but suddenly, you're never alone. Used to be people went out to dinner together. Now they go separately, and one of them comes and stays with you. Forget the bathroom. "Shave your legs? Over my dead body." They used to knock at a door, but now they just stick their head in to "see how you are." They think a head doesn't count, not like walking in with a whole body. For a whole body, they'll knock, but a head they'll send along unannounced. Count. You can reach four sentences in any conversation before the other person brings it up, "I'm really sorry about unintelligible mumble." And if *they* don't, you do it yourself, out of some perverse guilt. "Yes, I'm the one, yes, it was razor blades on the wrist. Gillette. Yeah they still make them. It's actually more ecological than using disposable blades. Yes, it did hurt. So badly that it made me really want to live." Letmeoutletmeoutletmeoutletmeout. Everybody wants to talk about it. Fine, let 'em, but what they mean is they want *me* to talk about it. In a group. Go over and over it, and every other flawed detail of my over-long existence. And I must listen to others. Failed in life and failed in death. A cry for help? Yes, in some cases, yes. A big cry of "Look at me, I'm in pain." That is so optimistic. "Look at me,

I'm in pain, and I think it will go away if I only take the right pill, meet the right person, get the right job, win lotto." I don't think for a second it will get better, I just screwed up, I screwed it up, everybody was supposed to be away for the weekend but there was a bomb scare and they all came back to our place to have a party. I screwed up the party too. They were so surprised; nobody was expecting it, nobody knew. And that's the problem, they think because they didn't know that anything was wrong then, why should they think that something isn't wrong now. So, here I sit, practicing until I get it right, or they get bored: "Listen. I'm not going to do it again. I'm not, I'm not. I'm really not."

Contributors

Jo J. Adamson has seen her plays produced in Seattle as well as Portland and Los Angeles. *Bread and Circuses* won the Grand Galleria Prize at the Pacific Northwest Writers Conference, and her full-length play, *The Wax Cradle*, was just published by Drama Source. Her poetry, short stories, and articles have appeared in literary as well as general interest magazines. Her special interest is in writing about women who have been ignored or glossed over in history books. She is a member of the International Center for Women Playwrights and the Dramatists Guild.

Dori Appel has written thirteen full-length plays, plus sixteen one-acts, shorts, and monologues, which have been widely produced throughout the United States and Canada. She received the Oregon Book Award in Drama in 1998 for *Freud's Girls*, and in 1999 for *The Lunatic Within*. She is also the winner of the 1994 New American Comedy Contest, the 1998 Crossing Borders Content, and the 1999 George Kernodle One-Act Play Competition.

Paula Cizmar's plays have been produced Off-Broadway, in London, and in theatres from Maine to California. She is the recipient of many honors including an NEA grant and a Rockefeller Foundation residency at Bellagio, Italy. Her plays include: *Candy & Shelley Go to the Desert, Still Life with Parrot & Monkey*, and *Street Stories*. She is a member of Echo Theatre Writers Unit and Circles Rising, an offshoot of a Paula Vogel Bootcamp at A.S.K. Theatre Projects in Los Angeles.

Heidi Decker is a Seattle-based actress and playwright. Her works include: *Small Mercies, Eye of the Beholder, Voices*, and *The Agony and the Irony*. When not in a theatre, you can find her on the ice, proud to be a goaltender for the Seattle Women's Hockey League.

Christina de Lancie wrote and directed the short film, "A Larger Night," which was featured in the Edinburgh International Film Festival, the Chicago Film Festival, the San Sebastian Film Festival, and Women in Film, Los Angeles. It received gold and silver awards. *F-64*, her first stage play, was workshopped at Carnegie-Mellon, received the 1992 Jane Chambers Playwriting Award, and was a finalist for the

1993 Susan Smith Blackburn Award. *Tsunami,* her second play, has received a reading at The Women's Project in New York.

Sandra Dempsey, youngest of twelve and born of proud Irish-Canadian ancestry, is an internationally recognized playwright and performance-reader. She has been elected as the first President of the International Centre for Women Playwrights. Her works include: *Armagideon* (Grand Prize winner, "New Play Search 99" Firefly Productions, Honorable Mention 1999 Jane Chambers Playwriting Award, and winner 1996 Alberta Playwriting Competition), *D'Arcy* (Finalist, Ontario Playwrights' Showcase), *Enigma* (Finalist, 1983 Broadcloth International Women's Playwriting Competition), *Barbie and Ken,* and *Per Ardua.*

Mindi Dickstein's plays and musicals, including *Guadeloupe, The Existential Gourmet, Dreaming Rita, The Falling Man,* and *Beasts and Saints,* have been produced or developed at Westbeth Theater, Women's Interart, Theatreworks USA, Cucaracha Theater, Second Stage, ASCAP Workshop, Musical Theatre Works, and the Vineyard. Her work has won the Jane Chambers Award and the Bernice Cohen Award and has been honored by Wendy Wasserstein/PEN International.

Elizabeth Nell Dubus writes plays, novels, and short fiction. Her play *Slow Fugue Before Dying* won the 1997 Festival of Firsts, placed first in the Aonian Productions Competition, and second in the Alleyway Theatre Maxim Maxumdar Competition. *Welcome Party* has been a finalist for national competitions including that of the National Repertory Theater and Futurefest. Her newest play is *Jazz at Midnight.* She is a member of the Dramatists Guild and the Authors Guild.

Linda Eisenstein's plays include *Three the Hard Way* (winner, Gilmore Creek Playwriting Competition and published by Dramatic Publishing*), Marla's Devotion* (Festival Prize, All England Theatre Festival), *The Names of the Beast* (winner, Sappho's Symposium Competition), and the monologue collections *Bad Grrrls.* A two-time Ohio Arts Council fellowship recipient, she is a member of the Cleveland Play House Playwrights' Unit. Her work has been widely produced in the United States, Australia, England, and Canada.

Annie Evans currently writes for the children's television shows *Sesame Street* (two Emmy Awards) and *Oswald the Octopus* on Nickelodeon. Her other plays have been produced at such theatres as Actors Theatre of Louisville, Manhattan Class Company, New York Stage and Film Company, Circle Repertory Company, the Ensemble Studio Theatre, The Lab, New Georges, the Westbank Café, and The Eugene O'Neill National Playwrights Conference. She is a graduate of Brown University.

Carolyn Gage is a lesbian-feminist playwright and performer. Her collection of plays, *The Second Coming of Joan of Arc and Other Plays*, was a national finalist for the Lambda Literary Awards, and her musical *The Amazon All-Stars* is the title work in Applause Books' lesbian anthology. She has written the first book on lesbian theatre production, *Take Stage! How to Direct and Produce a Lesbian Play*, as well as *Monologues and Scenes for Lesbian Actors*.

Terry Galloway is a writer and performer who writes and performs. She's written and performed four full-length solo pieces, hundreds of cabaret skits and monologues, and just recently completed a two-hour musical tragedy in burlesque, *In the House of the Moles*. She's received grants and awards from the usual suspects. She lives in the part of Florida that is not Miami Beach.

Elizabeth Gilbert's plays include *Door Wolves*, *Effects of Thunder*, *Transmigration of Existence* (finalist, Jane Chambers Playwriting Contest), *Children of Other Mothers* (selected for presentation at the 5th International Women Playwrights Conference in Athens, Greece), *Tolstoy is Dead!*, and *Sweetie's Not*. Elizabeth is the artistic director of Women's Works in Houston, Texas, which supports the development of women writing for the theatre.

Magdalena Gomez recently completed a yearlong appointment as a Community Associate at the Five College Women's Research Center at Mount Holyoke College, where she began the development of a new play, *You Don't Look It*. She is playwright-in-residence with Enchanted Circle Theater. ECT, supported by grants from the NEA and Xeric Foundation, has commissioned her to write a futuristic adaptation of *Don Quixote*, entitled *Landscapes*, for a national tour.

Sara Hardy's plays have been performed in Britain, the United States, Canada, and Australia. Titles include: *Vita!—A Fantasy* (about the relationship between Virginia Woolf, Vita Sackville-West, and Orlando), *Virtually Ethel* (about the composer Dame Ethel Smith), and *Queer Fruit* (intertwined monologues concerning three women from vastly different times). Trained as a performer, Hardy's initial motivation for writing was to create good roles for herself. Born in Britain, she now lives in Australia.

Laura Harrington's plays and musicals have been produced regionally, Off-Broadway, and in Canada. Some recent credits include: *Resurrection* (Music: Tod Machover), *The Perfect 36* (Music: Mel Marvin), *Joan of Arc* (Music: Mel Marvin), *Marathon Dancing, Martin Guerre* (Music: Roger Ames), *Lucy's Lapses* (Music: Christopher Drobny), *Hearts on Fire, Babes in Toyland,* and a feminist adaptation of *Sleeping Beauty* (Music: Roger Ames). Ms. Harrington is on the faculty at M.I.T. Awards include a Bunting Institute Fellowship, the 1996 Clauder Playwriting Award, a Whiting Foundation Grant, a Massachusetts Cultural Council Award for Playwriting, the Joseph Kesselring Award for Drama, Opera America development and commissioning grants, a New England Emmy, and a Quebec Cinematique Award.

Barbara Homans graduated from Indiana University in 1949 and migrated to the Village in New York City, where she worked as a researcher for *Time* magazine (sometimes in the theatre section) and wrote short stories. One of her stories was published in *Discovery* in 1951. But, like many women of her time, she succumbed to marriage. She offers no apologies. She became the mother of five children and then the partner in a divorce. The children had to be raised. She raised them. Now she is writing again.

Daphne R. Hull's plays have been produced and developed in eleven states. *Eulogy: What I Would Have Said, Given the Gift of Articulation* was a top finalist for the Princess Grace National Playwriting Award and received Honorable Mention in the Jane Chambers Playwriting Award for 1999. It was produced as part of the 1999 Boston Theatre Works Unbound Festival. She is a member of the Dramatists Guild, the International Centre for Women Playwrights, and the Playwrights Forum.

Barbara Kahn has received the Torch of Hope Award for "lifetime achievement" (previously given to Terrence McNally and August Wilson) and the James Quirk Award for "memorable contributions to American theatre." Her work has been seen widely throughout the United States, including New York. She is also an actress and director who has worked in New York, Paris, at London's National Theatre, and on tour. She is a member of Actor's Equity, Screen Actors Guild, and the Dramatists Guild.

Judy Korotkin is a published novelist (*The Spotlight*). She earned membership in the Writers Guild of America, West for an ABC after-school special that she wrote, and four TV movie options followed. Her short plays have been produced by Eccentric Circle Theatre and Love Creek Productions in New York, as well as by Actors Forum in Los Angeles. Her full-length play, *Wedding Pictures*, was produced by the 42nd Street Workshop in 1996.

Sherry Kramer's work has been seen at theatres across America and abroad, including Yale Repertory Theatre, Soho Rep, EST, New York's Second Stage, and The Woolly Mammoth. She has received NEA, New York Foundation for the Arts, and McKnight Fellowships, and has won the Weissberger Playwriting Award and a New York Drama League Award for *What a Man Weighs*, the LA Women in Theatre New Play Award for *The Wall of Water*, and the Jane Chambers Playwriting Award for *David's Redhaired Death*.

Sahra Kuper is from Boulder, Colorado. Her play *Under Covers* was part of the WordBRIDGE Playwrights Laboratory (1999) and was runner-up for the Kennedy Center American College Theatre Festival, the Jane Chambers Playwriting Award, and the Denis Johnston Prize. She is currently working on a book of short stories and living in Jamaica Plain, Massachusetts.

Shirley Lauro's work includes: *Open Admissions* (Broadway production, *New York Times* "10 Best Plays" list), *A Piece of My Heart* (Off-Broadway production, Kittredge Award, Barbara Deming Prize, finalist for Susan Smith Blackburn Prize), *The Contest* (National Foundation for Jewish Culture Award), *Margaret and Kit* (finalist for Jane Chambers Award), and *Pearls on the Moon*, from which her monologue here is taken. She has received fellowships from the Guggenheim, the NEA, and the New York Foundation for the Arts.

Dinah Leavitt, Fulbright Scholar and 1999 Colorado Arts Council Playwriting Fellowship recipient, is a professor of theatre at Fort Lewis College. Her *It's About Time*, from which her two monologues in this volume come, received a 1999 Jane Chambers Playwriting Award Honorable Mention. Author of two dozen produced plays, Leavitt wrote one of the first books on feminist theatre, *Feminist Theatre Groups*, in 1980.

Arden Teresa Lewis's play *Baby Dreams* was first produced at Theatre Ten-Ten in New York, then again as a Westworks production at

Theatre West in Los Angeles, and it was a finalist for the 1995 Jane Chambers Playwriting Award. Her play *Little Rhonda* was produced at Theatre Geo in Los Angeles. Excerpts of *Little Rhonda* have been published in *Scenes for Women by Women* (Heinemann). Her most recent play, *Grandma Good*, won the 1999 Lillian Nesburn Award from the Beverly Hills Theatre Guild.

Carol K. Mack's plays include *In Her Sight* (which premiered at Actors Theatre of Louisville's 21st Humana Festival in 1997) and *The Accident* (staged by American Repertory Theatre in 1995). Her other award-winning plays have appeared internationally and at American Place Theatre and EST in New York. Published plays include *Postcards & Other Short Plays*, *In Her Sight*, and one-acts included in *Best Short Plays of 1985, 1990*, and *1993–1994*.

Jennifer Maisel has won the California Playwrights Competition from South Coast Repertory, the Center Theatre International Playwrights Competition, the Roger L. Stevens Award from the Fund for New American Plays, and was a finalist for the Pen West Literary Award. She most recently received a New Play Commission in Jewish Theatre from the National Foundation for Jewish Culture. Her plays include *Mallbaby*, *Eden*, *Mad Love*, *Dark Hours*, *The Last Seder*, and *Animal Dreams*. She also writes for film and television.

Melissa Martin lives in Pittsburgh with her husband and three children. She has an M.F.A. in dramatic writing from the Carnegie Mellon School of Drama. Her plays (*The Shriveled Arm of Uma Kimble*, *The Last Bridge*, *Sow the Dawn*) have been produced regionally, in New York, and in Canada. She is at work on an independent feature film, which she wrote and is directing.

Mary Beth Maslowski is a fiction writer and journalist who is originally from New York City, but has also lived and worked in Japan, Hong Kong, and Germany. While she writes on a variety of subjects, issues relating to women especially interest her. Her fiction and nonfiction have appeared in *Salon* and *Women's International Net* magazine. In addition, her comedies and dramas have been performed in New York, Japan, and Germany.

Cassandra Medley's plays include *Ms. Mae* (one of the sketches which comprise *A . . . My Name Is Alice*), *Ma Rose* (staged by the Women's Project and Productions in 1990 and then throughout the United States; published by Samuel French), *Walking Women* (published in

Plays in One Act [1993]), *Dearborn Heights* (published in *Best Plays of 1995–96* and by Dramatists Play Service [1997]), and *Maiden Lane* (Ensemble Studio Marathon, 1999). She was awarded the Walt Disney Screenwriting Fellowship in 1990 for her screenplay *Ma Rose*. She also writes for daytime television.

Susan Miller won her second OBIE and the Susan Smith Blackburn Prize for her one-woman play, *My Left Breast*, which premiered in Louisville's Humana Festival. She has performed it in theatres around the country. Her plays *It's Our Town, Too; Nasty Rumors and Final Remarks; Flux; Cross Country; Confessions of a Female Disorder;* and *For Dear Life* have been produced by the Mark Taper Forum, Second Stage, Trinity Rep, and The Public Theatre, among others.

Rachelle Minkoff is a playwright whose works, *Bugaboo, Moment of Cruelty, Need, Triage, Fickin, The Cry, Scenes of Courtship and Family Devotion, The Widows, Solo, Go and Fetch and Fall and Break and Tumble, A Look of Glass,* and *Six Hundred Thousand Dead,* have been performed in New York, Boston, and Seattle. She teaches Writing for Performance at New York University, and resides in Brooklyn with her husband, Bert, and her son, Raphael.

Jill Morley began writing monologues as an auditioning actress who was too lazy to look through hordes of new plays. Now she is a writer who is too lazy to act. Her *True Confessions of a Go-Go Girl* was published in *Women Playwrights: Best Plays of 1998. Femonologues,* her collection of monologues, will be published in 2000. A regular contributor to the *New York Press* and *Shout!* magazine, she has also produced two radio documentaries for N.P.R.

Janet Neipris has had plays produced at theatres including Manhattan Theatre Club, Arena Stage (D.C.), Studio Theatre (D.C.), The Goodman Theatre (Chicago), Annenberg Center (Philadelphia), Milwaukee Rep, and the Pittsburgh Public Theatre. Chair of Graduate Studies, Dramatic Writing, at New York University, she is a member of the Dramatists Guild Council. Her plays are published by Broadway Play Publishing.

Penny O'Connor trained as an actor and worked with fringe theatre companies in London such as the Women's Theatre Group and the Half Moon Young People's Theatre. Her performed scripts include award-winners *Dig Volley Spike* (London, Chicago, New York) and *Bone Harvest* (Pentabus Arts, West Midlands). Presently, she is teaching the Alexander Technique at the ArtsEd London Schools and writing/teaching at her Greek Island home, which she shares with her partner, three cats, and a dog.

Sandra Perlman is an award-winning member of the Cleveland Play House Playwrights' Unit. This Philadelphia native has premiered more than a dozen plays in New York, Los Angeles, Chicago, and Cleveland. She is the recipient of two Ohio Arts Council fellowships in playwriting for *In Search of the Red River Dog* and *Cliff Diving*. She lives in Kent, Ohio.

Vivienne Plumb lives and writes in Aotearoa New Zealand, although she was originally born in Sydney, Australia. Her solo live art lecture, *Fact or Fiction: Meditations on Mary Finger (the Third in the Arnotts Iced Vovo Biscuit Lecture Series)*, has been invited to the 5th International Women Playwrights Conference in 2000. Her new novella is *The Diary as a Positive in Female Adult Behavior*, and her new poetry collection is *Avalanche*.

Lindsay Price divides her time between playwriting and working for her company, Theatrefolk, which sells original scripts to high schools around the world. Most recently, Lindsay was invited into Factory Theatre's Playwrights' Lab for the 1999–2000 season, and her play *Liver for Breakfast* was selected for performance by Pandora's Box in Buffalo.

Susanna Ralli is a playwright, editor, and actor in the Boston area. Her plays *The Cave* and *An Allergic Reaction* received staged readings at the Wellesley College Theatre. *An Allergic Reaction* and *Critique* were finalists in the Actors Theatre of Louisville National Ten-Minute Play Contest. *An Allergic Reaction* will be a featured play at the Annual Boston Theater Marathon and the International Women Playwrights Conference 2000 in Greece.

Deanna Riley's work has been produced Off-Broadway by Polaris Theatre North, in Richmond by Firehouse Theatre Project, in Milwaukee at Playwrights Studio Theatre Festival, and in Delaware by the City Theatre Company. Her scripts have won three regional Emmys: "Help Me, I'm Becoming My Mother!" (Best Entertainment Feature) and her contributions to "Crabs" (Best Entertainment Special for two years). Other awards include a Delaware State Arts Council Established Professional in Playwriting Grant.

Robin Rothstein's full-length play *On Deaf Ears* was produced Off-Broadway at the Kaufman Theatre, won a DGP's New Playwright Award, and was a finalist for the Jane Chambers Playwriting Award. Her ten-minute play "Thirty" was a finalist at Actor's Theatre of Louisville. She has performed her sketch comedy at Caroline's and HERE, among other venues, and is currently assembling a collection of her short plays. She is a graduate of the University of Pennsylvania.

Leah Ryan's plays have been produced in New York, Chicago, San Francisco, and London. She is a graduate of the University of Iowa's M.F.A. Playwriting Workshop and a member of the Julliard Playwrights Program. She also has a regular column in *Punk Planet* magazine and edits her own 'zine, *Violation Fez*. She is currently curating and editing an anthology of the service industry.

Tammy Ryan is represented in the first and second volumes of *Monologues for Women by Women*. Her other plays include *Pig* (published by Dramatists Play Service), *Vegetable Love, The Boundary*, and *The Music Lesson* (winner of the 1999 IUPUI National Playwriting for Youth Bonderman Award). She is a recipient of numerous playwriting fellowships from the Pennsylvania Council on the Arts and lives in Pittsburgh where she teaches playwriting.

Gwendolyn Schwinke is a playwright, teacher, and actor from Missouri who currently resides in Minneapolis. Her plays include *Ithaca* and *Thrown by Angels*, which was commissioned by Red Eye Collaboration and developed with additional support from The Playwrights' Center in Minneapolis. She is a past Associate at The Playwrights' Center and the recipient of the Center's Jones Commission. She holds an M.F.A. in Acting from Illinois State University.

Lisa Diana Shapiro is a writer/actor whose hit comedy, *Labor Pains* (about a gay Italian man and a straight Jewish woman who are having a baby together), premiered in Los Angeles and then played regionally throughout the United States. Her other plays have won awards in several national play competitions. She is a graduate of the Northwestern University theatre department and cohabits with an African Grey parrot who can quote Shakespeare.

Lillian Ann Slugocki has been writing, producing, and developing original award-winning programs for radio, television, and film for over fifteen years. She won the NFCB Silver Reel for *The Erotica Project* for WBAI Radio (presented at HERE and The Public Theatre/Joe's Pub) and for *The Archaeology of Lost Voices*, a thirteen-part historical series for National Public Radio. Other projects include an adaptation of *Mad Women for Modern Times, The Great Days of Witchcraft, Girl Trouble,* and *Epiphanies.*

Donna Spector's plays (*Another Paradise, Caught in the Act, How to Be Really Jewish, Strip Talk on the Boulevard, Hanging Women, Dementia,* and *Dancing with Strangers*) have been produced Off-Broadway, Off-Off-Broadway, regionally, and in Canada. She received two National Endowment for the Humanities grants to study in Greece and a grant from the Geraldine R. Dodge Foundation to produce her play *Not for the Ferryman.* She is a member of the Dramatists' Guild, Poets & Writers, and Harbor Theatre in New York City.

Diane Spodarek is an actor and award-winning playwright, video artist, poet, and fiction writer. Born in Canada and raised in Detroit, she lives in New York City with her daughter Dana. Her plays include *Happy Hour, No Smoking, Neutron Bomb,* and *The Drunk Monologues* (her one-woman play, from which "Men & Cars" is excerpted). She is the recipient of an NEA grant and three New York Foundation for the Arts Fellowships.

Caridad Svich is a playwright, translator, and songwriter affiliated with the Mark Taper Forum in Los Angeles, where she previously held an NEA/TCG Residency. She is coeditor of *Conducting a Life: Reflections on the Theatre of Maria Irene Fornes* and *Out of the Fringe.* Her plays include *Alchemy of Desire/Dead-Man's Blues, Any Place But Here, Pensacola, Prodigal Kiss, The Archaeology of Dreams,* and *Gleaning/Rebecca.* She has taught at the Yale School of Drama, Traverse Theatre (Edinburgh), and Paine's Plough (London), among other places.

Mary E. Weems is an award-winning performance poet and playwright and a doctoral student in Educational Policy. "Two Sides to Every Story" is excerpted from her full-length play *Another Way to Dance,* which addresses how fictional and real-life women from diverse backgrounds plot their own courses through patriarchy. Other plays include: *Dirt, Move to the Back of the Bus,* and *To Be or Not to Be in the 90s.* Her poetry collections include: *White Blackeyed,* and *Fembles.*

Erin Cressida Wilson is an internationally produced and award-winning playwright and Professor of Playwriting at Duke University. Recent projects include an Off-Broadway production of *Hurricane, The*

Trial of Her Inner Thigh at Camp Santo with Intersection for the Arts (DramaLogue and Glickman Awards), *The Erotica Project* (co-written with Lillian Ann Sluglocki) at Joe's Pub at the New York Shakespeare Festival, and a musical adaptation of her play *Cross-Dressing in the Depression* with Jack Herrick of the Red Clay Ramblers.

Y York's plays are produced with something approaching regularity at adult and all-ages theatres across the country. *The Last Paving Stone, Afternoon of the Elves, The Garden of Rikki Tikki Tavi, Accidental Friends,* and *the Portrait the Wind the Chair* are published by Dramatic Publishing. *Rain. Some Fish. No Elephants.*; *The Secret Wife*; *Gerald's Good Idea*; *The Snowflake Avalanche*; and *Life Gap* are available from Broadway Play Publishing. She has won the Berrilla Kerr Playwriting Award and the Joe Callaway Award from New Dramatists. She lives with Mark Lutwak, to whom most things are dedicated.

Performance Rights

c/o Heinemann:

Jo J. Adamson	Daphne R. Hull	Sandra Perlman
Dori Appel	Barbara Kahn	Lindsay Price
Paula Cizmar	Judy Korotkin	Susanna Ralli
Heidi Decker	Sahra J. Kuper	Deanna Riley Cain
Sandra Dempsey	Dinah Leavitt	Leah Ryan
Elizabeth Nell Dubus	Arden Teresa Lewis	Gwendolyn Schwinke
Carolyn Gage	Melissa Martin	Judy Sheehan
Terry Galloway	Mary Beth Maslowski	Donna Spector
Elizabeth Gilbert	Rachelle Minkoff	Diane F. Spodarek
Magdelena Gomez	Jill Morley	Caridad Svich
Barbara Homans	Penny O'Connor	Mary E. Weems

Christina de Lancie
c/o Peregrine Whittlesey
345 East 80th Street
#31F
New York, NY 10021

Mindi Dickstein
c/o Bruce Ostler
Bret Adams Agency
448 West 44th Street
New York, NY 10036

Linda Eisenstein
c/o Herone Press
P.O. Box 749
Cleveland, OH 44107-0749

Annue Evan
c/o Betsy Helf
William Morris Agency
1325 Avenue of the Americas
New York, NY 10019

Sarah Hardy
c/o Radclyffe Theater Productions
16-18 Barnett Street
Kensington, Victoria 3031
Australia

Laura Harrington
c/o Carl Mulert
Joyce Ketay Agency
1501 Broadway
Suite 1901
New York, NY 10036

Sherry Kramer
c/o Bruce Ostler
Bret Adams Agency
448 West 44th Street
New York, NY 10036

Shirley Lauro
c/o Peter Hagan
Gersh Agency
130 West 42nd Street
#2400
New York, NY 10036

Carol K. Mack
c/o Robert Freedman
    Dramatic Agency

1501 Broadway
New York, NY 10036
ATTN: Bob Freedman or Selma
    Luttinger

Jennifer C. Maisel
c/o Susan Schulman Literary
    Agency
454 West 44th Street
New York, NY 10036

Cassandra Medley
c/o Elaine Devlow
Luedky Associates
1674 Broadway #7A
New York, NY 10019

Susan Miller
c/o Carl Mulert
Joyce Ketay Agency
1501 Broadway
Suite 1908
New York, NY 10036

Janet Neipris
c/o Mitch Douglas
ICM
48 West 57th Street
New York, NY 10019

Vivienne Plumb
c/o Playmarket
P.O. Box 9767
Wellington, New Zealand

Robin Rothstein
c/o Ronald Gwiazda
Rosenstone/Wender
3 East 48th Street
4th Floor
New York, NY 10019

Tammy Ryan
c/o Ronald Gwiazda

Lisa Diane Shapiro
c/o Susan Schulman Literary Agency
454 West 44th Street
New York, NY 10036

Lillian Ann Slugocki
c/o Helen Merrill Ltd.
295 Lafayette Street
Suite 915
New York, NY 10012-2700

Erin Cressida Wilson
c/o George Lane
William Morris Agency
1325 Avenue of the Americas
New York, NY 10019

Y. York
Carl Mulert
Joyce Ketay Agency
1501 Broadway
New York, NY 10036